5minutemarketing

Mary Charleson, MBA

www.charleson.ca
www.fiveminutemarketing.com

For my mother, Nancy Holborn,
my lifelong guide and mentor.

And for my children, Alex and Pat.
May you also achieve your dreams.

Contents

Acknowledgements   ix

Introduction   xi

Chapter 1 Corporate Social Responsibility   1

That Consumer Green Shift Is No Marketing
Flash in the Pan   2

Corporations Discover Their Social Conscience   6

Brands That Give Back Get Back   9

New Ad Campaign Keeps Vancity Ahead of
the Enviro-pack   12

The Environmental Tipping Point   15

Survey Shows You Need a Social Strategy
for Your Brand   18

Selling Ethics and Advertising Can Build
Better Communities   21

Social Responsibility Advertising Riding
on the Wings of a Dove   24

Principles Important to Successful Marketing
Strategy   27

Chapter 2 New Media and E-marketing   31

Let the Digital Marketing Games Begin   32

Proliferation of DVRs Poses Challenge to
TV Advertisers   35

Marketing Budgets Not Keeping Up with
Digital Media   38

Marketing with Mobile Media   41

New Technology Affecting Media Channels
and How Marketers Interact with Customers   44

E-marketing Opportunities Continue to
Multiply in the Brave New Online World   48

Marketing on the Internet Is the New Prime Time   52

	Product Placement Now Interwoven in the Fabric of Media Marketing	55
	Gauging the Lower Mainland's Appetite for a Daily Dose	59
Chapter 3	**Marketing to Women**	**63**
	Nintendo Wii Fit Targets the CHO	64
	Did Lululemon's Mansy Joke Miss the Marketing Mark?	67
	The Power of Baby Boomer Women	70
	Reaching Men through Marketing to Women	73
	If You're Not Marketing to Women, You're Missing a Big Part of the Market	76
	Savvy Marketers Know How to Sell to Women	79
	Navigating to Venus and Mars	82
Chapter 4	**Advertising and Public Relations**	**85**
	Creating Media Buzz About Business Can Pay Dividends	87
	Are You Really Ready to Advertise?	91
	Good Advertising Means Knowing Your Target and Choosing Your Medium	94
Chapter 5	**Branding and Your Competitive Advantage**	**99**
	How to Give Your Brand an Enduring Competitive Advantage	100
	A Brand is More Than an Identity; It's a Promise to Deliver a Positive Experience	103
	Marketer of the Year: Vancity Offers a Case Study in Effective Marketing	106
	Former High-Flying Air Canada Hits New Marketing Low	110
	Brand Building Lululemon Style	113
	Brand Building 101	117

Successful Companies Define Core and
Supporting Strategies 121

Identify and Hone Your Competitive Advantage 125

Chapter 6 Marketing Planning and Strategy 129

Why You Need to Create a Personal Marketing Plan 130

The Seven Habits of Successful Marketers 133

Time Is Your Customers' Most Valued Currency 136

SFU, GM Get Good Mileage Out of
Business Project 139

Successful Business People Have Common
Traits and Behaviours 143

Westjet Soars on Its Price-Leading Strategy 146

Privacy Legislation Raises Public Issues
for Business 150

Chapter 7 Research 155

A Customer Who Complains Can Be a Business
Owner's Best Friend 156

Customers Really Do Know Best, So Talk
to Them! 159

Staying on Top of Business Trends Helps
the Bottom Line 163

Lower Mainland Companies Use
Environmental Scanning to Keep a Step Ahead 167

Competitive Intelligence Builds Base for
Business-Winning Strategy 171

Chapter 8 Sales 177

Simple Sales Tips from a Successful
Five-Year-Old 178

Sales Lessons from the Long, Winding Road 181

Speak Up: It Could Be Your Best Marketing Move 184

Full Sale: Marketing's Seafaring Similarities 187

For Success Stories, Starting at the Ground
Floor, Ready Your Elevator Pitch 190

Four Currencies Add Up to Better Business
Results 193

Chapter 9 Trends 197

Big Ideas About Thinking Small in an Era
of Consumer Uncertainty 198

Sins, Staples, and Small Pleasures on
Consumer Wish Lists 201

Credit Card Call Highlights Consumer
Vulnerability 204

Marketing Financial Services Offers Host
of 21st-Century Opportunities 207

Poll Surveys Consumer Views on Income
and Debt 210

In the Modern Marketplace, Time Is the
New Currency 213

Playing the Value Game Is Vital in the New
Shift-to-Thrift Era 216

Baby Boomers Are Leading the
Shift-to-Thrift Trend 219

Consulting Services, Presentations, and Keynotes 222
Satisfied Clients Get the Last Word 223

Acknowledgements

■ ■ ■

I have always enjoyed writing, but it wasn't until I completed an MBA as a working adult that I decided to become published. During the graduation ceremony, we were challenged to find something valuable to do with the extra time we had created in our schedules to complete our graduate degrees. I committed at that moment to writing some articles on marketing to submit to the business weekly near where I live. The editor accepted one of the samples for print, and then to my surprise, sent me an editorial schedule for the next year. That was seven years ago, and since then, I have written a great deal on marketing-related issues. Additional pieces have appeared in national marketing magazines and city dailies across Canada. That work became the content for this book. It needed to be shared.

Thanks to Ian Noble, who gave me my first column in 2002, and to Tim Renshaw, my current editor at *Business in Vancouver*. I'd like to thank Dan Poynter for his advice in the preparation of this book as well as Elaine Allison and Donna Hutchinson for encouragement in realizing this lifelong goal. Thanks to Arlene Prunkl, my editor, for her tireless demands for perfection; Naomi Pauls for her proofing detail; and Victor Crapnell for the fabulous cover design. I'm grateful to the clients and businesses that shared their stories. And finally I'd like to thank my family - my husband, Chris, and my children, Alex and Pat, who engage my daily observation and discussions on marketing, and Nancy Holborn, my mom and lifelong mentor, who has always been my inspiration.

Introduction

. . .

This book is for people who want to learn about marketing through Canadian case studies and examples offered in a short article format. It can be read in its entirety or by topic area. Each article can be read in five minutes or less and will give you valuable marketing insights that you can put to work in your business right away.

I emphasize business examples because I believe that is the most effective way to understand marketing concepts. Many of these pieces first appeared in *Business in Vancouver*, where I have been a monthly columnist since 2002. Other pieces have appeared in *Marketing Magazine, Strategy Magazine, Marketline*, and the *Toronto Star* newspaper.

These short articles have been arranged by theme rather than chronological date of publication. Each themed chapter features an overview and update on any relevant issues since the article was first published.

If you are interested in more marketing ideas and insights, visit my blog at www.fiveminutemarketing.com. For consulting and speaking engagement information, as well as to sign up for my e-newsletter, *Marketing Rapport*, visit www.charleson.ca.

CHAPTER 1

Corporate Social Responsibility

■ ■ ■

I first wrote about ethics and the attention some companies were paying to the impact of their corporate soul on their employees after interviewing Ann Coombs in 2003, author of *The Living Workplace*. Perhaps slightly ahead of her time in 2001 when her book was first published, Ann certainly had identified a key ingredient that would emerge as a leading social trend in marketing later in the decade.

Social strategy and its influence on how customers form an emotional connection with your business or your brand is the single most important marketing insight today. Based on my past research with Pollara and recent research with TNS Canadian Facts, talking to people right across Canada, I don't think this is just a trend, or something apt to go away quickly. I suspect the importance of social strategy will likely only deepen, given the broad interest across all demographic groups and a propensity for social responsibility to become even more important with age.

Brands that have a social strategy as one of their core founding values will have an advantage. As the field gets crowded with companies jumping on the philanthropic bandwagon, it will also become harder to use this as a differentiating strategy. Soon it will be seen simply as the way business is done. And as the recent financial crisis places pressures on expenditures, the companies that continue to have social responsibility as a core message will realize significant competitive gains.

That Consumer Green Shift Is No Marketing Flash in the Pan

■ ■ ■

Business in Vancouver newspaper, September 30, 2008

The game has changed. There is a huge market shift taking place. I just heard a radio commercial offering $15,000 off the price of an SUV. A discount of $15,000? It wasn't long ago you could actually buy a vehicle for that. Stay tuned; I'm waiting for the one where they *offer you* $15,000 to take it away.

In June of 2008 GM announced it would halt production at its pickup truck plant in Oshawa, Ontario, and close it in 2009. They also planned to close three other plants that assemble SUVs. "We at GM don't think this is a spike or a temporary shift. We believe that it is, by and large, permanent," said Rick Wagoner, chairman and CEO of General Motors. He also said they were reviewing the future of the expensive Hummer brand. Clearly they have an incredibly firm grasp on the obvious with that move.

Fluctuating gasoline prices are changing consumer behaviour and rapidly affecting the auto industry sales mix. This change also comes at a time when the US is still reeling from the subprime mortgage fiasco and the effects of the consumer debt rippling through the economy. Although Greater Vancouver has seemed somewhat isolated from these fears, economic effects are filtering through Canada, particularly in manufacturing-heavy Southern

Ontario. There's nothing like fear and threat as a stick to provoke change.

Sustainability, environmental consciousness, going green, doing good, authenticity; they're all words and phrases that swept into our vocabulary over the last year. The continued spike in fuel prices has just served to elevate the issue daily. We have the light green and the dark green camps to define the degree of environmental action consumers take in their lives. We have greenwashing to describe the unscrupulous act of wrapping your marketing message in green while your internal policies are shallow or claims unsubstantiated. With so much buzz on the issue, I was starting to worry that interest might have peaked and that from a marketing perspective, all the buzz about environmental and social causes could turn into a flash trend. I couldn't have been more wrong.

Recent cross-Canada research from TNS Canadian Facts indicates that interest and action in this area continues to grow at a staggering pace. We engaged in a research study to compare attitudes year over year on this issue. The results were startling. Raymond Gee, senior researcher at TNS Canadian Facts, notes: "You may think it's reached a plateau, but it hasn't. These issues aren't going to die down. The interest continues to grow." Results were gathered through a phone survey of one thousand Canadians in May 2007 and May 2008. The margin of error was 3.1%. Here are some of the questions with analysis.

Have you ever switched from one brand to another that was about the same price and quality, because the other brand was associated with a more socially and environmentally responsible company?

	2007	2008
Overall:	45%	58%
Men:	41%	51%
Women:	48%	65%
35 - 49 yrs	40%	65%
BC residents	51%	63%

"Past behaviour is a good predictor of future behaviour. When almost 60% of people say they have switched for this reason, that is a significant result," remarks Raymond Gee. "I don't know of any business that can afford to lose 60% of their customers." The movement of 10 to 15% up across all categories between 2007 and 2008 is also very significant. Women in particular are quick to switch. Regionally, BC is one of the most sensitive areas.

I consciously choose to do business with companies that are socially and environmentally responsible.

	2007	2008
Overall:	37%	50%
Men:	33%	46%
Women:	42%	55%
35 - 49 yrs	28%	58%
BC	45%	54%
Vancouver	45%	58%

Movement is significant across the board. Of particular interest is the 30% jump in the thirty-five to forty-nine-year-old, prime consumer category. BC and Vancouver results were the highest in the country.

I feel businesses mislead customers with overstated environmental benefits.

	2008
Overall:	35%
Men:	37%
Women:	33%
35 - 49 yrs	38%
BC residents	38%

We didn't ask this question last year, but it has become evident consumer leeriness is growing around the integrity of businesses touting leadership on this issue.

What will become painfully obvious in the coming year is that there is a fundamental shift happening. It's here for the long term. Concern for social and environmental issues has quickly gone from being a fringe marketing positioning issue, one that could be used as a point of differentiation, to becoming the price of entry for business.

Corporations Discover Their Social Conscience

■ ■ ■

The Toronto Star newspaper, August 8, 2007

Have you noticed a trend lately? Companies are donating profits to good causes. Charities are hooking up with brands. Brands are launching their own causes. Environmental issues are going mainstream. Call it caring, call it compassion; consumers are saying they value the impact that business has on the world. It appears that doing good is now good for business. But why the shift? Why now?

What is absolutely remarkable is the fact that a couple years ago we were scarcely having the discussion. The environment was largely a fringe concern. Giving back was limited to charity sponsorship and philanthropic contributions. Now we have brands like Dove aspiring to evoke social change by challenging the stereotypical view of beauty. Toyota is staking claim as an environmentally forward car manufacturer. Home Depot has launched over a thousand Eco Options products designed to be gentle on the environment. One could argue that all this has the makings of a flash trend, but that would be a serious mistake. In fact, this change has been coming for some time. Three factors are contributing to this social and environmental shift:

1. Rebound from corporate greed
We all witnessed the scandal surrounding companies like Enron, Nortel, and Martha Stewart. What has become painfully evident is that accountability now matters. These scandals awakened a giant within. Shareholders and consumers are voting with their wallets, and Corporate Conscience became a bottom line issue.

2. Powerful weather events
We have been rocked by weather events worldwide. Before hurricanes in the south, water shortages in Europe, and drought in Australia, the National Weather Service graph of severe weather events in the United States rises like a ski jump over the last forty years. Clearly something is not right. It took last winter for many North Americans to hit the tipping point. What they saw around them, coupled with the phenomenal successes of Al Gore's Inconvenient Truth presentation, raised the platform. People began to talk.

3. Demographic shifts
But this third factor is the most powerful one. Recent research conducted across Canada by TNS Canadian Facts and research in both Canada and the United States by Youthography show interesting demographic trends. There are three key insights:
    (1) This trend is incredibly strong with youth. Those under twenty-five care a lot about this issue. When asked if they consciously choose to do business with companies that are socially and environmentally responsible, 41% of those eighteen to twenty-four years old agreed in Canada. When asked if they would consider buying environmentally friendly products, 49% of fourteen to twenty-nine-year-olds in Canada agreed, while 34% of Americans felt the same way. This group has powerful ideals, they

are wired, and they are empowered to change the world. Their baby boomer parents told them that they could do anything. Now they seem poised to do just that. Coming into their greatest years of influence, they are the largest demographic group since the boomers.

(2) The second demographic factor to consider is aging baby boomers, many now over fifty. Moving into a stage of life where they begin to consider legacy and their impact on the world, they too care a lot about this issue. In fact, the passion for this issue is distributed like a reversed bell curve, rising the highest with youth and those over fifty. The boomers represent a huge target group with incredible wealth and influence. When asked if they consciously choose to do business with companies that are socially and environmentally responsible, 43% of those over fifty years old agreed.

(3) And finally there is the incredible power of the female consumer, buying or influencing 80% of purchases. That woman with a purse skews significantly higher than men for sensitivity to environmental and social concerns, with 42% of women and 33% of men consciously choosing socially and environmentally responsible companies. The numbers rise significantly in boomer women with 57% of women, over fifty making this choice.

Clearly social and environmental responsibility is no flash fad. The societal trend and demographic optics indicate it has traction. Perhaps the flight to corporate consciousness and sustainability will in fact be sustainable.

Brands That Give Back
Get Back

■ ■ ■

Strategy Magazine, May 2007

There can be little doubt. There is a movement afoot and it's called social strategy. Consumers are saying they value the impact that business has on their world. Good corporate citizenship now matters. Recent polling of 1,200 people across Canada by Pollara, Canada's largest polling, firm reveals proof:

> 71% of women and 57% of men said they don't mind paying more for products that are produced in an environmentally responsible manner.

> 81% of women and 72% of men said they believe the time has come to deal with environmental sustainability.

> 73% of women and 66% of men said they are more apt to buy a brand that gives back to the community. This escalates to 90% for women from thirty-five to fifty-four years of age.

> 84% of women and 76% of men said it is important to deal with businesses that make the world a better place through their actions. 80% of people in Greater Toronto said it was important to them.

> 62% of women thirty-five to fifty-four years old said that an ad that demonstrates social responsibility resonates with them. There was an education and income skew. The higher the education or income, the more this mattered. "We've noted in our research

that women tend to be more passionate about social responsibility and become more so as they get older, where men tend to stay the same as they age. That said, these numbers indicate that social consciousness is important to both men and women," notes Michael Antecol, VP, Pollara.

It is important to keep in mind that social strategy needs to be at the heart and soul of a business, and not applied like philanthropic lipstick at the end. When it is part of the very essence of the brand, it breeds a profound emotional connection with consumers.

Having a social strategy may well be the latest buzz, but brands where a social strategy has been at the core of their brand promise since inception long ago realized the power it can yield. For those genuinely social conscious brands, it was more about sharing customer values than becoming a successful brand. When it's honest and those shared values make an emotional connection with customers, good brands become great brands. They own a distinctive position in the marketplace and often keep their customers for life.

Just look to the success of Mountain Equipment Co-op. Their core values state: "We conduct ourselves ethically and with integrity. We show respect for others in our words and actions. We act in the spirit of community and co-operation. We respect and protect our natural environment. We strive for personal growth and continual learning." "These aren't just words," notes Peter ter Weeme, former manager of communications and marketing at MEC. "It's what we actually deliver." And they just happen to have sold $225 million in products for wilderness recreation pursuits this year doing it. Ter Weeme, who recently launched his own company, Junxion Strategy, recognized the social strategy trend. Junxion Strategy helps businesses with their commitments to sustainability and social marketing.

Vancouver-founded Vancity Credit Union is another great example. They are driven by a triple bottom line of financial returns, social returns, and environmental returns. Their brand promise is "Balanced prosperity." Vancity CEO Dave Mowatt states, "We make a profit because we do good things. We don't just do good things to make a profit." They donate 30% of profits to members and the community each year. Last year that was $12 million. They award $1 million annually to an organization supporting a social, environmental, or community project. Their Enviro-Visa contributes 5% of member spending to support environmental causes. They have Clean Air Auto Loans at a reduced rate to support the purchase of hybrid vehicles. And their Bright Ideas home loan supports improvements to lesson environmental impact.

Consumers are increasingly searching for sources of meaning and trust. They're looking deeper, and they're turning to brands that support their values and connect with them on an emotional level. Having a social strategy now matters.

A note to readers: Dave Mowatt left Vancity in June 2007. Tamara Vrooman is now CEO. Michael Antecol has since left Pollara and is now VP, TNS Canadian Facts.

New Ad Campaign Keeps Vancity Ahead of the Enviro-pack

■ ■ ■

Business in Vancouver newspaper, July 20, 2007

So where does a company take its advertising when the green turf of social and environmental responsibility it has occupied starts to get crowded?

How does it continue to differentiate itself when these values, at the core of its brand DNA, become more common? Vancity's recently launched brand campaign, which will continue to roll out during the balance of this year, goes a long way to answering those questions. Canada's largest credit union, with $12.3 billion in assets and fifty-six branches throughout the Lower Mainland, Fraser Valley, and Victoria, Vancity is driven by a triple bottom line of financial, social, and environmental returns.

This year's campaign, created by TBWA Vancouver, has a more fun-loving, cheekier, and personalized tone than past advertising, which leaned on inspirational messages to establish authenticity. And that seems to be where Vancity is one step ahead with this campaign. Where other new entrants to the environmental and social responsibility movement need to establish credibility, most often through earnest and thoughtful messaging, Vancity has moved on to humour within this serious message as a point of differentiation. This option could be available only to an established player. "From a strategic point of view it's good that everyone is getting in and addressing these issues," said Sloan Dinning, Vancity's director of brand and marketing communications. "But from a brand point of view, we want to stay ahead. We've earned the street credibility on this issue to not be seen as offering window dressing."

The new "We All Profit" campaign theme explains why Vancity does all the things it does. "We fundamentally believe we can help our members profit personally and help the communities they live in," said Vancity's marketing vice president, Kari Grist. "This year's campaign reinforces the notion that with a triple bottom line approach to everything we do, we all profit, and it communicates a point of difference in a humorous, yet smart manner."

The new campaign unleashes Vancity's everyday creativity and innovation and demonstrates it through both products and services that set it apart through an innovative execution. You'll see Western Canada's first solar-powered billboard in early July along Expo Boulevard. It will serve not only as a brand-positioning icon, but also as a testament to Vancity's commitment to environmental sustainability. A completely transparent bus shelter will advertise its transparent business practices. Vancity's unique mixer mortgage, which enables groups of people to buy a house, will be advertised with humorous TV and online spots. One TV spot features four people in bed, an irreverent and humorous illustration of the shared mortgage. Other TV and online spots feature bad behaviour in a bathroom with aerosol cans and a couple in an ice igloo that appears to be melting from global warming. Both spots position Vancity as environmentally astute while offering innovative mortgage solutions. Transit shelters' message, "For hard core environmentalists who can't stop buying shoes," will help promote Vancity's Enviro-Visa, a credit card through which 5% of members' spending is donated to environmental causes. Guerrilla marketing efforts include a bike share program launched this past week, to get more people out of their cars. YouTube and Facebook postings will encourage online word of mouth to augment the initiative. A micro website (www.weallprofit.com) has been launched to educate visitors about how Vancity initiatives realize profit on many different fronts.

The new campaign elements work collectively to draw attention to Vancity's values. And the use of humour and a quirky approach help them stand out in the increasingly crowded field of marketing with a social conscience.

A note to readers: Sloan Dinning has since left Vancity for career opportunities in Australia, and Kari Grist is now VP of marketing and business dedvelopment at Offsetters. The current VP of marketing at Vancity is Richard Seres.

The Environmental Tipping Point

■ ■ ■

Business in Vancouver newspaper, March 5, 2007

Malcolm Gladwell's book The Tipping Point poses a number of theories about why certain social phenomena take off while others are relegated to obscurity. He calls the tipping point "that magic moment when an idea, trend, or social behavior crosses a threshold, tips, and spreads like wildfire." For anyone interested in marketing, and the influence of society for social or financial gain, it is an intriguing read.

I figure the environment hit a tipping point on or around December 27, 2006. That was the day I tried to but couldn't rent Al Gore's An Inconvenient Truth. My local Rogers Video store reported that all their copies were out, and that the number being returned was dwindling. Customers were simply choosing to keep the movie and pay the penalty. Retailers were sold out. In the east they were kayaking on the Rideau Canal, and we were recovering from windstorms. Mother Nature had spoken, and it seemed we were finally listening.

In subsequent months the media and conversations were littered with environmental coverage. The environment was and still is hot, literally, and with a recent poll placing it as the number one concern among Canadians, even politicians are now waking from their slumber. Seems the colour to wear this spring will be green.

There are many reasons to look at sustainability in your business practices. Beyond the social, emotional, and environmental benefits of doing so, it also makes good marketing and business sense. In January 2007, I asked Pollara, the survey company, to survey 1,200 people across Canada on this issue. Our goal was to get feedback on environmental issues from a marketing standpoint. On whether they believe the time has come to deal with environmental sustainability, 82% of university graduates agreed, while agreement dropped to only 62% for those with no post-secondary education. 81% of women and 72% of men agreed. Women across all age groups had similar levels of agreement as did men from eighteen to thirty-five years, at 80%. However, support by men dropped with age to 69% for men over fifty-five years. Interestingly, Quebec is passionate about this issue. 82% in the province agreed, which was the highest of all Canadian provinces, followed by British Columbia and Ontario at 78%. Both urban and rural respondents shared the same level of support.

On whether they would pay more for products that are produced in an environmentally responsible manner, those with higher education and higher incomes were more apt to agree. 71% of those earning $75,000 or more agreed and a further 36% agreed strongly. The results skewed female, with 57% of men thirty-four to fifty-four years agreeing, while 70% of women in that age group agreed. 73% of women over fifty-five agreed and a further 42% strongly agreed.

"The numbers are high all around, but there is a gender effect. Women seem to be more passionate about social and environmental issues, and become more so as they get older," notes Michael Antecol, VP, Pollara. BC and Quebec gave the highest support, both at 71%, while the prairies and Alberta were the least concerned, at 48% and 55% respectively. So are Canadians ready to buck up to support environmental initiatives?

"Yes, they are," says Michael Antecol, "and depending on who you target and where you conduct business, there are some pockets of greater opportunity."

Junxion Strategy, a Vancouver company focused on social and environmental sustainability marketing, has caught the updraft of this trend. "The appetite is there in a way I haven't seen in years. It's moved to the boardroom. Six months ago versus now is huge. It's moving so fast," says Peter ter Weeme, principal. He notes the environmental initiative of large corporations such as GE and their Ecomagination program with products such as eco-friendlier jet engines, bio gas engines, wind farms, and photocells as examples.

"GE has invested in things that link to their traditional offerings in an environmentally sustainable way," notes ter Weeme. "Junxion also does work around internal branding and employee retention. Youth want their work to represent the whole person. They don't want to check their values at the door," he says. Given the support of youth for environment-related issues and the coming labour shortage, there is a strong case to push for sustainability.

Upholstery Arts is a home furnishings company going green. They now offer a whole line of furniture made of wood certified by the Forest Stewardship Council of Canada. They also offer product take-back, where you can return your purchase for reuse or recycling. Birks' recent pledge to use no "dirty gold" in support of the Canadian Boreal Initiative is another example.

From an internal and external branding perspective, environmental and social sustainability seem to be the way of the future. Customers and employees are demanding it. Are you ready to deliver?

Survey Shows You Need a Social Strategy for Your Brand

■ ■ ■

Business in Vancouver newspaper, October 24, 2006

Have you noticed a change taking place in business? Charities are teaming up with brands. Companies are supporting good causes. Environmental issues are becoming mainstream. It would appear that corporate consciousness is growing. Often it's altruistic and sometimes it's about brand building, but undeniably it's because business has realized that consumers are demanding it.

Businesses where a social strategy has been at the core of their brand promise since inception long ago realized the power it can yield. For those genuinely social conscious brands, it was more about sharing customer values than becoming a successful brand. When it's honest and those shared values make an emotional connection with customers, good brands become great brands. They own a distinctive position in the marketplace and often keep their customers for life.

Let's look at some research on just how powerful this need for a social strategy has become. I recently undertook a study with Pollara, the Canadian national public opinion and market research firm. In a poll of 1,206 people across Canada we asked: 1. How important is it to deal with companies that care about the community they conduct business in? 2. How important is it to deal with businesses that make the

world a better place through their actions?
3. Does an ad that demonstrates social responsibility resonate with you?

Survey result highlights:

On the importance of dealing with companies that care about the community they conduct business in: 87% of women and 78% of men said this was important to them. These are strong numbers. They get even higher, up to 90% for women aged from thirty-five to fifty-four years. These numbers are a real heads-up if you sell to women. Although the movement seems strongest in the Atlantic provinces, 80% of British Columbians said it was important to them.

On the importance of dealing with businesses that makes the world a better place through their actions: Again women are consistently higher than men. 84% of women and 76% of men agreed. Curiously, 80% in Greater Toronto said it was important to them, while 66% in Greater Vancouver said it was. Intuitively we think of the west coast as the heartland for this stuff. It's where the co-op style business model used by successful companies such as MEC and Vancity has been enormously successful. Perhaps it's fall-out from corporate greed in a head office town. Alternatively, maybe those on the coast just take social responsibility for granted by now.

On whether an ad that demonstrates social responsibility resonates with them: The female skew remained consistent here. Baby boomer women in particular, those thirty-five to fifty-four years old, care a lot about this. There also appeared to be an education effect. The more highly educated, the more the respondent was apt to care. Upper and middle-income earners cared the most, while those with low income or those with very high incomes cared much less.

What does it all mean? It means having a social strategy is important. And if your business targets customers where the sensitivity to the issue is elevated, it is even more important. Just look to the success of locally founded Mountain Equipment Co-op. Their core values state: "We conduct ourselves ethically and with integrity. We show respect for others in our words and actions. We act in the spirit of community and co-operation. We respect and protect our natural environment. We strive for personal growth and continual learning."

"These aren't just words," notes Peter ter Weeme, manager of communications and marketing at MEC. "It's what we actually deliver." And they just happen to have sold $225 million in products for wilderness recreation pursuits this year doing it. Consumers are increasingly looking deeper, and they're turning to brands that support their values and connect with them on an emotional level.

A note to readers: Ter Weeme, who has since launched his own company, Junxion Strategy, recognized the social strategy trend. Junxion Strategy helps businesses with their commitments to sustainability and social marketing.

Selling Ethics and Advertising Can Build Better Communities

• • •

Business in Vancouver newspaper, August 22, 2006

We in the marketing industry spend our days advising clients on how to persuade consumers to buy things, part with their money, and make our cash register sing. Although many advertising campaigns are sincere and clever, there are ones that tap insecurities, reinforce oppressive stereotypes, and create needs out of wants. It can make for some pretty shallow stuff if one is left to ponder the relevance amid political turmoil, war, and destruction.

Enter ethical advertising. At first glance it may appear an oxymoron, but there is an afterthought of a growing desire to make the world a better place. And it's starting to make inroads in the field of advertising. Maybe it's a backlash response to the lack of control over world affairs. Maybe it's pent-up idealism and guilt shared by boomers now emerging from their blind consumer-driven youthful years. Maybe it's the emergence of a new generation of demanding, knowledgeable, ethically focused youth. Whatever is driving them, conscious consumers are on the rise. And with them comes the emergence of advertising that uses its power to not only persuade and help stimulate sales, but provoke healthy discussion and social change. Three examples:

Vancity's "Change Everything" campaign: Launched this past summer, the campaign will run in waves all year. "You can change everything if you change your bank" is the theme of the new ad campaign. It challenges people to make banking choices that will have a positive impact on their communities in addition to their wallets. The ads highlight Vancity's community and environmental focus. Highlighted are programs such as Shared Success, in which Vancity gives 30% of its of its earnings back to the community and its members; the Clean Air Auto Loan, featuring discounted financing for hybrid cars; and the Enviro-Visa, which donates a percentage of profits to environmental issues chosen by the cardholder. Street marketing efforts will see teams with video cameras film people talking about what they would like to see changed in the city or their lives. The filmed clips will be broadcast on a blog and invite customer feedback. "Change Everything invites people to change the way their money works. It's about how people can effect large change by making a small change like switching their credit card," says Sloan Dinning, Vancity's director of marketing communications.

Diane Lund is president and creative director of Creative Wonders, a Vancouver advertising agency specializing in communications for businesses interested in balanced, enlightened living. She notes, "Creativity guided by conscience is a healthy and sustainable way to approach marketing." The Vancity campaign is a great illustration of that.

The Dove Campaign for Real Beauty: This global multi-platform campaign set out with a lofty goal to change the definition of beauty. Now in its third year, the campaign taps into the need for women to be considered attractive no matter what their perceived flaws, and it challenges the narrow stereotypes about what is beautiful. It takes aim at the status quo and works to change perceptions. The real beauty of the campaign is that it has gone beyond the core target group - anyone can identify with its honesty. The brave step this campaign took has set the stage for others. Addition Elle, a clothing store for women size 14-plus recently featured a new campaign, "Curves make the woman." Full-figured women are shown in scantily clad self-confident poses. Again recognizing that women have long been the subject of stereotypes, it challenges the lack of self-confidence women may feel when their body doesn't live up to societal pressures.

Mountain Equipment Co-op: As a retail co-operative, MEC serves the needs of its members and is a force for positive social and environmental change. What little advertising they do positions them in this light. Their products are built with purpose, people, and the planet in mind. They pioneered green buildings, a recent trend to improve the communities in which we live. When locally based MEC expanded to the Toronto market, they constructed a "green building." Comprising 70% reused materials, the design also required less energy to operate.

So amid the shallowness of the pure pushing of product there are some shining lights that show how clever marketing can blend with social responsibility. Not only can it contribute to a better society, it can also produce bottom line results. That's the kind of profit we can all live with.

Social Responsibility Advertising Riding on the Wings of a Dove

■ ■ ■

Business in Vancouver newspaper, May 30, 2006

Advertising has the power to move and compel. It can persuade and position. And sometimes it can even aspire to evoke social change. A lofty goal, but one Dove has set since launching their "campaign for real beauty" to counter the negative self-esteem influences of perfect body images used in fashion and cosmetics advertising to young women.

A Harvard University study conducted globally with 3,300 young girls and women indicated that more than two-thirds of those surveyed expressed that they strongly agreed with the statement "Media and advertising set an unrealistic standard of beauty that most women can't ever achieve." Nine out of ten respondents wanted to change something about their body. And 67% said they withdrew from everyday activities because they felt badly about the way they looked. Only 2% of women felt comfortable describing themselves as beautiful. These statistics are shocking and shameful. As the study indicates, it is a fair assumption to connect media and advertising influences as a contributing factor to unrealistic body image expectations. And that is where socially responsible marketing and advertising requires sober second thought. Enter Dove and the "campaign for real beauty."

In September 2004 Dove launched their campaign with an evocative series of ads. They featured real women and unconventional beauty on billboards. Boldly showing no product and minimal branding, freckles, wrinkles, and curvy bodies were placed in the spotlight. It was a definite departure from what others in the fashion and cosmetics industry were doing. Dove made themselves vulnerable and had women talking. By questioning the accepted definition of beauty, the goal was to help women change the way they perceive their bodies and encouraged them to feel beautiful every day.

The campaign was so successful that the brand has experienced double-digit growth in every category. And the success continues. Current ads feature real women with real bodies and real curves. The campaign is intended to celebrate diversity by challenging today's stereotypical view of beauty. Although the company no doubt desired sales and market share increases, the "campaign for real beauty" has gone far beyond driving the bottom line. Those involved want to drive actual social change. In fact, Janet Kestin, co-chief creative officer, Ogilvy and Mather, Toronto, the agency responsible globally for the brand, states emphatically, "Dove is a movement. We are creating a cult."

The brand's commitment to inspiring positive self-image among women has extended to initiatives that support a wider definition of beauty. The Dove Self-Esteem Fund was launched in spring 2005 to help teach young women about self-esteem issues. Mentors work with schools and Girl Guides to deliver the "True You" program, featuring a book of activities to provoke dialogue on self-image issues between young girls and their female mentors. Dove has also partnered with NEDIC, the National Eating Disorder Information Centre, to help promote a healthy body image.

The Dove "campaign for real beauty" as a global effort is intended to serve as a starting point for societal change and act as a catalyst for widening the definition and discussion of beauty. "It takes thirty years to realize social change," says Sharon MacLeod, marketing manager, Dove master brand, Unilever Canada, "and we are committed to our approach."

Other businesses have ventured into this field to a lesser degree. The Reitmans "real fashion for real life" campaign featured clothes conceived, designed, and priced for real women, not runway models. The campaign depicts real women as they actually live. The quirky approach of strutting like a fashion model down the runway of life, getting on a bus, doing laundry, going to work, buying groceries, or picking up the kids, struck a chord with women. The media buy used print, billboards, and TV. It was funny and it was a departure from the ordinary. It poked fun at the fashion industry and it was seen as authentic. Although we have yet to see the brand's long-term commitment to this approach, it does represent movement toward a responsible ideal.

Can marketing and advertising evoke and support social change? Time will tell. But as marketers we should recognize the power that media can yield, and the ability we have to support these efforts.

Principles Important to Successful Marketing Strategy

• • •

Business in Vancouver newspaper, July 1, 2003

Your company's values, what you stand for, and what your people believe in are crucial to your competitive success. But are your company values reflected in your marketing strategy? You've likely addressed the four P's of product, price, place, and promotion, but what about the fifth P, that of *principles*? In a world of fallen business icons, both employees and customers harbour distrust. Customers are seeking comfort and connection. Employees want their workplace to be a reflection of who they are. Where there is conflict, poor communication, or a lack of leadership with principles, it radiates outwardly to customers. Leading companies have leveraged their position in the marketplace by capitalizing on their values in their marketing strategy. The key is, they must be authentic.

Ann Coombs, president of Coombs Consulting Ltd. and author of *The Living Workplace*, believes there are a few CEOs and visionaries who succeed in putting values and soul into the workplace. "These individuals understand human behaviour, maintain a position of overall corporate well-being, and balance the integrity of employees with the need to make profits," she says. Coombs Consulting, founded in 1980, studies consumer trends, provides strategies, and conducts think-tank and change management programs. Ann has become increasingly disturbed at the prevalence of what she calls the "toxic workplace."

"A toxic corporation is focused exclusively on short-term productivity and profits without equal concern for the hearts and souls of its workers," she explains. "As we enter the twenty-first century, we are carrying an attitude towards an employee as a disposable replaceable tool rather than a human being with soul, spirit, and heart." She believes the toxic environment is becoming the standard rather than the exception. It is with the publication of her book, *The Living Workplace* (www.livingworkplace.com), her international speaking engagements, and her consulting practice on this very topic that she has found her own passion and purpose. She has worked with Envision Credit Union, the Pan Pacific Hotel, and Rocky Mountaineer Rail Tours, all of whom she considers to have made putting values in the workplace a priority.

Envision Credit Union, Canada's third-largest credit union, with branches throughout the Lower Mainland and the Fraser Valley, was ranked among the fifty best companies to work for in Canada by the *Globe and Mail's Report on Business* magazine. The results were based on evaluations by staff of things such as leadership, value of staff opinions, career development, and employee benefits. Gord Houston, CEO, notes, "This is an affirmation that we believe in people first." A philosophy of exceptional member service, a desirable work environment, and commitment to community involvement is at the foundation of their success. Employees participate regularly in community events sponsored by Envision, and the company supports many local and regional nonprofit organizations. They contribute over a half million dollars a year to communities in which they operate.

Clearly there is marketing leverage in their positioning. They have aligned stakeholder interests with company interests. They strive for leadership with integrity. They are focused on customers' interests. They value employees as team members, and they are part of their community. This positioning has value because it is authentic. Notes Gord Houston, "It was interesting to see bottom line CEOs open up about their values during a recent Coombs ideas lab for our board. We are flexible and adaptable toward innovation and value input from our people. I expect one new idea will net us $2 million/year." Now that's getting value from your values!

Kimberly Locicero, director of innovation at the Pan Pacific Hotel, had Ann Coombs work with her leadership team. "The travel industry has faced so many external challenges such as SARS and terrorism, that we realized our staff was under a lot of pressure. We did not want our core values to become threatened and reflect outwardly to customers. Keeping an inward focus on our principles has become an extension of our outward marketing strategy. We practice six core values: caring, respecting and empowering our people, uplifting communities, achieving business excellence, and balancing local and global markets. "Ann helped us open up and communicate our concerns, so we could truly practice our values," Locicero notes.

Rocky Mountaineer Rail Tours, founded in 1990, is the largest privately owned passenger rail service in North America. They feature daylight railtours of scenic BC and Alberta from April to October, with seasonal departures in December and January. With 70,000 guests per year, they are one of the top rail trips in the world. Graham Gilly, VP, Marketing, notes they offer a truly international product, with 85% of guests coming from outside Canada. "Our vision is to provide the most spectacular experience in the world, to guests, employees, suppliers, and partners," says Gilly. They analyze consumer data from the 30,000 comment cards received annually and know that 98% of guests felt their expectations had been met or exceeded. They recognize that consistent staff structure and training is the key to delivering superior guest services. "We aspire to be a preferred place to work and structure our environment and values to attract and retain the best employees," notes Gilly. The 95% return rate on seasonal positions gives them consistency and continuity and is a testament to their success at putting values and soul in their workplace.

Ann Coombs says that what sets these companies apart from others in their pursuit of success is the authenticity and intent in incorporating values in the workplace. They also strive to keep their business models and marketing strategies open to adaptability and flexibility.

Are authentic values and principles worth pursuing in business? Yes. Can they be leveraged to position you well in the marketplace? *Absolutely*. Putting the "P" for principles in your marketing strategy will benefit your business, your staff, and your customers. Plus, it's simply the right thing to do.

A note to readers: Rocky Mountaineer Rail Tours is now Rocky Mountaineer Vacations, part of the Armstrong Group.

New Media and E-marketing

■ ■ ■

After the initial infatuation with all things online, and then the subsequent dot.com crash, we seem to have come to our senses about how to use e-marketing effectively. We knew there was amazing potential; it just took some time to creatively leverage how to use it effectively. There is some truly exciting stuff happening with electronic marketing, and it will only grow exponentially over the next several years. Web 2.0 applications, interactive and user-generated content, social networking, blogging, and seeded online video have changed the face of online marketing. Traditional media aren't going to go away anytime soon, but they will never be the same as they once were. Media consumption habits will change, and with that will come shifts in media buying. Growth will come in direct, targeted, one-on-one communication, and in the areas of collecting and filtering content for a profiled end user. New opportunities will emerge and traditional vehicles will struggle to remain relevant to survive. Electronic marketing is positioned perfectly for growth in this area. It's a brave new world out there!

Let the Digital Marketing Games Begin

■ ■ ■

Business in Vancouver newspaper, February 11, 2009

The last fifty years have been about mass marketing and one-way communication. But consumers have changed and many don't trust advertising anymore. They've been lied to and faked out. Ads have become like wallpaper - seen but not remembered. And consumers have become savvy. Media can no longer be the cracks between the content. Enter digital marketing. Digital is the ultimate mass and individual marketing all at once. And because digital content is social, encouraging connections between people, it becomes the content.

The future of advertising? There isn't any. Well, not quite. But the future of traditional advertising vehicles will not look like the past. Although billboards, transit, TV, radio, print, and direct mail ads will still be present, they'll be used to create synergy with digital media in some form. Progressive companies are currently doing this in growing numbers and with measurable success, an attribute likely to foster further growth, with increasing pressure to justify advertising return on investment. We are entering a time when marketers are simply assessing their objectives and target markets, then selecting the best tools for the job, be they traditional, digital, or a combination of both.

Petro-Canada's recent Olympic glassware promotion is a great example of how integrating online and traditional media can reap huge success. With a nod to the past, the thirty-second TV commercial states, "It was 1988, the Calgary Winter Games, when the country came together to support Olympic athletes, with glasses," says the voiceover. "Isn't it time to do it again?" It continues, "Buy the glass and support Canadian athletes, only at Petro-Canada." The voiceover and music audio is reminiscent of a homey Hotel 6 spot, as it pans the cupboards and garage shelves where some of those 1988 glasses now reside.

The use of TV is obviously aimed at mass reach, likely best to connect with Canadians over thirty-five. But they also utilized social networking through Facebook for an online campaign. The company offered free "virtual" versions of the glasses that Facebook users could send their friends as gifts. Petro-Canada donated fifty cents for every virtual glass passed along to support Canada's Olympic athletes. Their goal was to donate $50,000. Their gift-giving number spiked to 70,000 in the first day, and they had achieved their goal of 100,000 virtual gifts within three days. Most of the Facebook givers were women drivers aged eighteen to thirty-four. The online campaign was aimed at creating buzz for the actual glassware that retails for $3.99 - half of which is donated to support Canadian athletes. The Facebook application allowed them to connect with individual Canadians, then use their personal network of friends to share the content to a mass number of people. Brilliant.

Forgetting Sarah Marshall, a romantic comedy launched last year that followed Peter after being dumped by Sarah, utilized both traditional and digital media in a clever way for its launch. They could have just posted a movie trailer to YouTube, bought print ads, and waited at the box office. Instead, they embarked on a transit campaign as a teaser to drive people to the website. Bus ads stated, "My

Mom always hated you, Sarah Marshall." Transit ads went further: "You do look fat in those jeans, Sarah Marshall." Each ad posted a website at the bottom. Once at the website, people could get to know Sarah and Peter, learn each side of the story, look at posted photos and video and exchange thoughts and advice through the website and blogs. As a teaser campaign, it was not known to be a movie at that point. People thought they might be engaging in relationship advice for a real couple, albeit one with a messy, public, and expensive media-glorified breakup. The point is, traditional media drove traffic to the web, where viewers then followed the story and engaged with others using social media. When the movie actually launched, they had already become participants in the story and of course they went to see it. The movie grossed over $100 million globally.

The future of advertising? There is one. It just doesn't look the same as in the past. And you can count on it engaging digital media in some capacity.

Proliferation of DVRs Poses
Challenge to TV Advertisers

• • •

Business in Vancouver newspaper, March 11, 2008

The digital video recorder (DVR) is changing all the rules in the advertising game. That's the nifty little device most shops will insist on selling you when you ante up for that new plasma or LCD flat-screen TV that has relegated perfectly functioning black-box TVs to an electronic wasteland. The digital video recorder allows viewers to stop, start, pause, and record TV viewing. Seamlessly simple compared to its VCR cousin, which required a degree in manual reading and untold patience, the DVR allows viewers to record and effectively time-shift television viewing at the push of a single button. A show, once recorded, will be subsequently recorded and saved to the hard drive every time it is broadcast in the future. Being stuck downtown at a meeting or dutifully appearing at your child's school talent night needn't be such a sacrifice. But the scary part, at least for advertisers and those who make money in the TV ad business, is the ability of this little electronic box to allow viewers to skip through commercials.

The DVR is no longer just for affluent early adopters, although this group is certainly well represented. According to February 2008 research across Canada just completed by TNS Canadian Facts, 38% of all Canadians own a DVR. Ontario has the highest penetration at 41%, while BC was 39%. Forty-five percent of those eighteen to twenty-four years and 39% of those thirty-five years old and older own a DVR. Forty-six percent of those earning over $80,000 own one. In a very short period of time, this technology has permeated our homes, arriving primarily on the back of the flat-screen TV revolution.

According to Josh Bernoff, VP and analyst, Forrester Research, Boston, 60% of programs viewed, where DVR technology is present, are recorded. When recorded shows are later viewed, 92% of ads are skipped. "This reduces ad exposure by 54%. This is the incontrovertible math that tells you TV advertising can't stay the way it has been. The thirty-second commercial is going to be a victim of this math," says Bernoff.

"The percent penetration number from TNS Canadian Facts seems extremely high to me," notes Andeen Pitt, media director at Wasserman and Partners. "I have not heard anything like that number. I think Nielsen is reporting the US at 20% penetration and Canada is slightly behind. It is intuitive that the younger age group, more likely to be early adopters and frankly also those who spend a disproportionate amount of their income on electronics, will have a higher penetration rate. Over time this will balance out," notes Pitt.

The Bureau of Broadcast Measurement (BBM) pegs overall household penetration of DVRs in Canada at 12 to14%. Carmen Hunt, media director at TBWA Vancouver, says, "Although the TNS numbers seem a bit high, I wouldn't be surprised because in Canada we are more urban. We've adopted broadband much quicker than elsewhere in the world."

Raymond Gee, senior research associate at TNS Canadian Facts, stands behind the research but notes the discrepancy may be due to methodology. "I have no reason to doubt BBM's numbers.

Our research was conducted through an online panel of 1,020 Canadians. People we interviewed have more access to the Internet, broadband connections, and cable and ultimately will be more tech savvy. The numbers will be higher than in a phone or mail-back survey," notes Gee. Regardless of how you view the numbers, there is a story emerging here that paints a very interesting picture within the growing tech-savvy Canadian population.

The bottom line, says Carmen Hunt at TBWA Vancouver: "It's not simple anymore. Trying to do advertising in creative ways is challenging. With the way TV is viewed, we've always emphasized frequency because people can leave the room when commercials come on. This is really no different. The exciting thing for us is that people with DVRs are actually consuming more content. If it's an offer of interest, or the creative is really strong, they'll watch. This has also opened doors for branded content, product placement, and in program advertising."

I'm convinced there is something genetically linking men and remotes, and with this little gem of technology now on their side, advertisers who target young males and affluent households will have their work cut out for them. Stay tuned, and don't touch that remote!

Marketing Budgets Not Keeping Up with Digital Media Consumption

■ ■ ■

Business in Vancouver newspaper, April 8, 2008

Last month we looked at how the digital video recorder (DVR) was changing the rules of the TV advertising game. This month we take a more in-depth look at numerous technology-driven activities that have proliferated in modern-day life, to measure their impact on marketing efforts.

We looked at the time spent social networking online, visiting virtual worlds, writing emails, blogging, talking on a cell phone, video gaming, watching DVDs, going to movies, watching TV, reading, and listening to music. We wanted to get a sense of where people were spending more, the same, or less time on these activities compared to a year ago. TNS Canadian Facts conducted the research through a cross-Canada panel of 1,000 respondents in February 2008.

Overall, there were three things we are doing more of: social networking, writing emails, and listening to music. Although there were variations across demographic groups, all these areas experienced an increase. There are two things we are doing less of: blogging and watching TV.

Thirty-seven percent of females and 28% of males said they were spending more time social networking online. There was a definite youth skew to the results: 51% of those eighteen to twenty-four and 42% of those twenty-five to thirty-four years old said they were doing more of this activity. In BC 27% were spending more time social networking.

Thirty-three percent of females and 29% of males said they were spending more time writing emails. The majority, 54%, said they were spending the same amount of time on this activity as they had a year ago. The number of people spending more time stayed relatively consistent across age groups. Perhaps BC is a little more relaxed after all, since 25% here reported spending more time on this activity compared to 38% spending more time in Ontario.

Although cell phone use was about the same for the majority of groups, one group stood out. Thirty-one percent of those eighteen to twenty-four years old reported spending more time on this activity.

Listening to music was on the increase. Overall 26% of respondents reported spending more time on this activity. Again youth stood out. Forty-four percent of those eighteen to twenty-four reported spending more time on this activity.

Overall 72% of respondents said they had never blogged. Eleven percent said they were doing less, 8% said they were doing the same, and 4% said they were doing more.

Although 61% overall said they were watching the same amount of TV, only 15% said they were watching more, and 22% said they were watching less. Twenty-eight percent of those eighteen to twenty-four years old were watching more TV. This was the only group with a significant increase in viewing habits. However, it is still the older demographic, those over fifty years of age, who are watching the most TV overall.

So what does it all mean for marketers? While Canadians may be spending less time watching TV, we appear to be shifting our habits toward online activities such as social networking and emailing as well as listening to digital music obtained online. Although the shift is most dramatic for younger audiences, consumers across all demographics are increasing the amount of time they spend consuming digital media. But marketing budgets have been slow to align with consumer habits. Forrester Research estimates that the average North American spends 20 to 30% of their media consumption time in digital channels. Yet they report that ad agencies on average spend approximately 12% of budgets on digital media. Marketing budgets appear to be out of line with consumer habits.

The story to grasp here is that the growth in the amount of time spent with digital media is real and will continue to grow over time. Many businesses are recognizing this and changing their advertising and marketing allocations accordingly, but a gap still exists.

Marketing with Mobile Media

■ ■ ■

Business in Vancouver newspaper, May 8, 2007

The world of cell phones is abuzz with activity these days. Telus narrowly missed a consumer revolt over their nearly ill-fated foray into downloadable porn. Announced without fanfare, guided by greed, and flying in the face of any corporate social strategy, it's hard to believe this initiative was planned to roll out less than a month before call number portability came into effect. Of course, now all providers are tripping over themselves to spread the love. With all the new capabilities of mobile technology out there, could it be that there is more at stake than making and receiving a few phone calls? You bet!

There is an entire industry dedicated to making your cell phone do more. Much more. It's called mobile media. Leora Kornfeld, co-founder of Ubiquity Interactive, sees a cell phone as more like a remote control for your personal entertainment system. Ubiquity's system, MetroCode, is a cell phone-based mobile arts and entertainment service that radically extends the capability of a cell phone. It lets you use your cell to browse and activate your surroundings. Users dialing into their system can access a combination of professionally produced and user-created content ranging from audio and photos to text and multimedia messages.

The system launched in May 2006 with the Vancouver Sculpture Biennale, a public art festival featuring sculptures displayed in public places through April 2007. Viewers were invited to call a central phone number and enter a specific code for one of the twenty-two public pieces they were viewing. The feature enables a mobile-guided art exhibit, with the additional capabilities to leave and retrieve text messages, photos, and videos on a website and comments about the art. It has made art public, participatory, and interactive. The system has tracked approximately a thousand calls per month. This project was part of an industry-driven research initiative called Mobile MUSE (Media-rich Urban Shared Experience). The long-term vision is to develop MetroCode as a tourist product for the entire city by 2010.

For marketers, the possible commercial applications for this technology are intriguing. Last fall the Vancouver International Film Festival launched Mobile VIFF through ACM Media, as an experimental mobile interactive tool designed to give film audiences access to festival information through their hand-held devices such as cell phones, BlackBerries, iPods and other PDAs. "We are getting feedback from VIFF members right now. What we do know is that attitudes and understanding of mobile technology in Vancouver is behind Europe and Asia, but the initiative was generally well received," notes Keith Lay, the president and creative director of ACM Media.

Vancouver Opera is now using mobile technology as a marketing tool for the opera *Tosca*. A dial-up audio campaign is being promoted on transit buses, transit shelters, and posters. There are nine audio vignettes narrated by CBC's Gloria Macarenko, followed by music samplers and an invitation to buy tickets. "The singing posters offer a gateway into the thrill and intrigue of *Tosca*," says Doug Tuck, director of audience development and community programs at Vancouver Opera. "This project is helping us imagine new ways to communicate with our audience of today and tomorrow in a dramatic and fun way." Many people think they need a knowledge base to access opera. That's why this application is so interesting. It makes a poster a less static thing and offers a way in. Industry leaders see mobile media as a "third screen." "People have a personal and emotional connection with mobile media, more so than their desktop computer. They use it to access and share information. This makes the possibilities for marketing fascinating," says Kornfeld.

"Mobile media is poised for an expansion, similar to the explosion that the Internet had ten years ago, but it is hampered by user fees. Most people, most of the time, think about how much stuff costs before they try it on their cell phone. The 'pay per' model that the phone companies use is profitable, but unfriendly to both innovation and user," notes Richard Smith, associate professor, Simon Fraser University School of Communication.

In a world of mass advertising and increasingly cluttered message spaces, anything that offers customer engagement and one-to-one communication is very savvy. And in the future, content will be "pushed" and linked to online applications. Mobile media can increase the level of interest and engagement at the moment of contact. Rather than viewers seeing an ad and acting later or forgetting to act at all, mobile media can capture an actionable moment. And for marketers that can make the cash register sing.

New Technology Affecting Media Channels and How Marketers Interact with Customers

■ ■ ■

Business in Vancouver newspaper, May 8, 2007

New technology is dramatically affecting media channels and how marketers interact with customers. That was the predominant message made at the recent BCAMA (BC chapter of the American Marketing Association) VISION Conference. Think back for a moment to 1997. *The English Patient* won an Oscar for best picture, Princess Diana was killed in a car crash, and eBay and Amazon were new and unknown. Microsoft owned the desktop, and Mac was on its way to extinction. Google wouldn't exist for another two years. Technology is doubling every twelve months. The way we approached marketing and advertising just ten years ago is very different than today. As a marketer it can be hard to keep up. New technology has altered the way companies choose to communicate with their customers. Consider these three changes:

1. Loss of the intermediary

The Internet has introduced a world where intermediaries are not required. In traditional advertising vehicles such as TV, print, and radio, the role of advertising was to interrupt and catch attention. A network or publisher controlled these media. Now online vehicles such as YouTube, MySpace, e-newsletters, blogs, and interactive websites are being used to connect conversations. Intermediaries used to control time and content. Now the consumer controls both content viewing and creation. This shift fundamentally changes not only what our advertising message should be, but also how it gets delivered. "There are 71 million blogs out there and 120,000 new blogs started every day," observes Mitch Joel, president, Twist Image. "Because of technology, individuals have a platform for a one-to-many conversation."

2. The empowered consumer
What used to be a one-way company-to-customer message has now become two-way. "The consumer is in control. They have equal voice. You can't outspend them to get noticed," says Mitch Joel. And technology has given consumers real power to effect change. Witness the recent move by the Forest Ethics environmental group to use Google Earth mapping software to produce video, subsequently posted to YouTube to show viewers West Fraser Timber Company logging operations the group felt were endangering caribou habitat in BC and Alberta. Or check out www.biggreenpurse.com, which is encouraging one million women to use the power of their purses to influence over 80% of purchases - to shift $1,000 of money they already spend to environmentally conscious products. Their goal is to have a $1 billion impact. Empowered and knowledgeable consumers are savvy and more resistant to marketing. This is your new reality. Bloggers have influence. You cannot control your message alone.

3. New media
New media such as YouTube and MySpace have given ultimate control of message and content to consumers. And it's not just

youth using these sites. According to Marketing Vox, half of YouTube's audience is over thirty-four years old. These vehicles are user driven, and although the production value on most YouTube spots is reminiscent of the early days when desktop publishing promised to make everyone a designer, viral word of mouth about entertaining spots spreads incredibly fast. Hunter Madsen, director of marketing, Yahoo Canada, explained a contest to launch Shakira's new album based on contestants submitting their own thirty-second music video for her "Hips Don't Lie" single. The marketing twist here was that they offered up Shakira's brand and asked consumers to do something with it. They gave their trust. The edited music video submissions were posted as a "mashup" on YouTube. The word of mouth promotion was incredibly effective and done at very little cost. "The traditional boundaries are getting fuzzy between creators and consumers," says Paul Lavoie, chairman and chief creative officer, TAXI. "New media offers us an opportunity. We're no longer telling and selling in advertising. We're relationship marketing."

"The cell phone has become a technology Swiss army knife," suggests Richard Worzel, Futuresearch. Consumers can text, send and receive email, browse the web, listen to music podcasts, view TV programs, play games, activate mobile message codes, and - oh yes - place a phone call. According to Juniper Research, the mobile entertainment market is forecast to reach $47 billion by 2009. Mobile devices make media accessible 24/7. "When new media arrives, the old media usually don't go away, but the way people use it changes," notes Richard Worzel, futurist. YouTube, Apple TV, TiVO, and DVRs have changed the way people view and use broadcast TV. Craigslist has changed the use of newspaper classifieds. E-newsletters have changed the role of direct mail. Blogs and citizen web reporters have altered the role of columnists and reporters. The old media didn't go away, but their use is being significantly altered. "Creating great content and experiences for consumers, that's where the future is, not advertising," notes Mitch Joel of Twist Media. Bold words? Yes, but right on target.

E-marketing Opportunities Continue to Multiply in the Brave New Online World

■ ■ ■

Business in Vancouver newspaper, July 17, 2006

The dot.com bust several years ago jaded even the most seasoned marketer on the promise of low-cost and quick return e-marketing. So infatuated were we with the promise of this new medium that we scrambled to apply all the tried-and-true methods that had worked in traditional vehicles like print and broadcast. Static banner ads, brochure-like websites, and non-interactive broadcast commercials largely failed to inspire. Only recently have we begun to truly appreciate the potential of electronic marketing with new innovative applications.

First some facts: According to Ipsos Reid, 78% of Canadians have access to the Internet and 72% have high-speed access at home. 85% of BC residents are online. 79% of Canadians voluntarily register with a website to receive permission-based mailouts, while the average Canadian will register with nine websites to receive commercial email. The average Canadian receives 164 emails a week; however, spam accounts for at least 50% of these.

Clearly there is potential. The challenge, of course, is getting noticed and remembered. So where to begin?

1. Permission-based email

It's time efficient, can save you money, and offers a targeted message to a pre-qualified audience. You can segment your customer base and response is trackable. However, getting your message read amid email clutter and spam filters can be a challenge, and opt-in, opt-out and bounced emails must be managed. But with an interested customer base, care to meet Canspam legislation, and respect for the amount of contact, permission-based email can be extremely effective. Just ask the Vancouver Opera. E-marketing has enabled a dramatic change in their business.

About a year ago the opera embarked on an aggressive plan to collect email addresses of attendees. Motivated by attractive prize incentives and an altruistic understanding of the implied savings in communication costs, 10,000 attendees are now on their email list. The opera wanted to communicate in a fast easy way, give special offers, provide traffic warnings and parking advice, save money on printing, and ultimately control their own ticketing. Not only have they succeeded in launching their own online box office, but they have been able to analyze a campaign and make adjustments. Jonathon Harrison, marketing director for Vancouver Opera, notes, "When there's an offer, we get six times the click-throughs."

2. E-newsletters:

Vancouver Opera educates and fosters community interest through a monthly e-newsletter. Sent once a month, the single page update is quick to read, comes in a graphically pleasing HTML format, and offers numerous website links throughout for more detail.

3. Interactive website content:

An interesting website innovation called Media Viewer allows the opera to film behind-the-scenes footage, interviews with the cast, clips of rehearsals, and audience feedback and then posts these immediately on their website. They have also utilized this feature to offer customers audio previews of the coming season.

Over at the Vancouver East Cultural Centre, there is also success with e-marketing efforts. While converting their mailing list to a permission-based e-list, there has been little opt-out action from participants. "Once people have opted in and we give them desirable information in a respectful manner, we generally keep them," says Duncan Low, executive director. "Using email and our website has been a great way to get our message out. It's much cheaper and more efficient than print." They too have utilized Media Viewer clips of audience reviews and posted them to their website following a show opening. Not only does it create a buzz about the event, it offers non-editorialized reviews, a bonus when short-run shows close before print reviews are published. Real people with real opinions available the next day could relegate the print review to obscurity.

4. Blogs and viral marketing

The Vancouver East Cultural Centre has successfully harnessed the power of blogs as a positioning vehicle. To help grow their youth market they developed a youth panel, a group who met bi-weekly and kept in touch electronically. They encouraged youth to create blogs for their youth week. Youth had complete content control. Individual blogs and links between them created a viral marketing opportunity. The VECC effectively gained an authentic voice with their target group by relinquishing control. The result was the most successful youth weeks ever, with very low promotional costs.

Viral marketing, essentially electronic word of mouth, harnesses the power of message pass-along, but with an implied personal endorsement, which is key. Easy-to-forward e-newsletters and emails, incentives to share with a friend or reciprocal website links can all form powerful methods of multiplying a message. The Vancouver Opera and the VECC have harnessed this in their e-marketing efforts. Both groups worked with YaYah Studios, a local design house with an affinity for the cultural arts and creative e-marketing flair to design and implement their campaigns.

There's a whole lot more than email spam and pop-up banner ads going on out there. Smart marketers are harnessing the power of e-marketing and with it driving the bottom line.

A note to readers: Heather Redfern has since replaced Duncan Lowe as the executive director at the Vancouver East Cultural Centre. Krista Constantineau has replaced Jonathon Harrison as marketing director for Vancouver Opera.

Marketing on the Internet
Is the New Prime Time

■ ■ ■

Business in Vancouver newspaper, February 5, 2007

The Internet as a medium for marketing promised to revolutionize the way we reach customers. After some initial missteps, largely caused by applying the old rules to a new game, we have emerged into an exciting era of possibilities. What seemed a futuristic forecast at best only a short time ago is now coming to fruition.

Where the advertiser had full control with traditional media, consumers now interact with content. It's now all about choice and control. And to be chosen, you must be innovative and interactive. "The Internet is the new prime time," says Hunter Madsen, marketing director for Yahoo Canada. "The Internet represents 20% of weekly media usage, but marketers currently spend only 6% of their ad budget on it." This imbalance is likely to change as marketers discover new ways to utilize the medium. A recent PricewaterhouseCoopers report, "How to Capitalize on Lifestyle Advertising in a Customer-Centric World," observes, "Convergence has blurred the lines between content, advertising, distributor, and consumer." The report advocates lifestyle advertising that allows advertisers to respond to consumer feedback in an interactive way through continuous dialogue. Personalized, participatory, socially interactive, relevant, and trustworthy are the signatures of effectiveness.

When Dove launched the Dove Self-Esteem Fund in Canada in 2005, their goal was to improve women's body image by educating girls on a wider definition of beauty. To build awareness, they created a TV commercial, "Little girls," which featured images of young girls with captions such as "Thinks she's fat" and "Hates her freckles". They placed the spots on TV shows like *Nip-Tuck* and *America's Top Model* to provoke discussion. The campaign generated a lot of talk and free media coverage. Great campaign by the old rules, but flash forward to the fall of 2006 and enter the Internet application. Dove filmed a digital commercial called Evolution, featuring a fast-forward view of makeup and touch-up techniques that turn the girl next door into a billboard model. The clip illustrates the impossible ideal that the beauty industry has created.

This time the spot was released on Dove's website and loaded on the shared content forum YouTube. In one month it received 2.3 million hits and was picked up on US talk shows, CNN, Fox, *Entertainment Tonight* and *Good Morning America*. Dove estimates it received over $50 million in free media. Strategic online placement was used rather than TV media placement. Viewers were pulled through viral word of mouth rather than having the message pushed at them during TV viewing. An accurate measure of views was achieved rather than an estimate of TV show viewers. And finally, online placement was free and the persuasive value of the media endorsement was priceless.

Yahoo has pioneered something they call behaviour marketing. By tracking demographics, geography, context, and behaviour of a Yahoo web search user, they can match advertisers' ads with individuals whose recent behaviours online suggest that those brands might be relevant to the person at this time. The service brings classic direct marketing tactics to an online application. Yahoo creates profiles by gathering behavioural data anonymously. Each profile indicates an area of product relevance on a particular day. They've determined an average purchase cycle for each product category and tied this into the length of time ads are displayed. Based on the frequency of searches, time spent browsing, and the type of material viewed, they further profile users as "engagers" or "shoppers." Advertisers pay on a cost per click basis, so the advertising is not only targeted, but also measurable. Although Yahoo declines to give figures, they do say revenues grew 450% last year. Hunter Madsen, marketing director for Yahoo Canada, also notes, "Most Fortune 500 companies are using or testing our system in the US. A travel company on our site which through traditional means had a $42 per customer acquisition cost now tracks at $7 per customer." This system arrived in the US in 2006. Watch for it in Canada in the next eighteen months.

The Vancouver East Cultural Centre conducts a regular email campaign to promote each show to past attendees. Built as an attractive HTML graphic template, the email enables the VECC to track who opens it, time spent, responses to offers, and clicks to their website. "We include filmed audience feedback from opening night to promote short-run shows where reviews often publish after closing," says Heather Redfern, executive director. This is a brilliant application. Their Internet-based campaigns have replaced large mail-outs of past. Communications are targeted, cheaper, and arguably more effective.

The recurring theme seems to be: engage your customer, know your audience, customize, measure, and track. The winners are those positioned to influence conversations around their brand. Welcome to the new game.

A note to readers: In August 2008, Hunter Madsen left Yahoo Canada as marketing director to become VP, Digital Media, BC Region, for Canwest Publishing.

Product Placement Now Interwoven in the Fabric of Media Marketing

∎ ∎ ∎

Business in Vancouver newspaper, February 5, 2007

Apple computers used in the TV series *24*, people meeting at Starbucks in a movie, or Best Buy being the featured marketing challenge on *The Apprentice*. This is product placement. From the overt to the unobtrusive, product placement is everywhere. It has become big business on the screen and in the media. Why? Consumers are inundated with advertising. While this fragmentation threatens the effectiveness of traditional advertising, product placement seeks to cut to the organic level by becoming "part of the story." When done well, brand-name items are used as props within the context of a movie to make it authentic and realistic. It is where the line between advertising and entertainment or advertising and editorial becomes blurred. Products can simply be chosen to enhance a scene, or they can be used by arrangement with either product or financial compensation.

The current trend in TV is to use a combination of the thirty-second commercial and product integration in the show. Coca - Cola has done this on *American Idol*. Product placement has made its way into movies, TV, video games, music, books, newspapers, and magazines. Just how effective is it in TV? Nancy Tear, founder of PropStar, a Vancouver product placement firm, declines to give exact figures but notes, "Getting Alienware Computers coverage on *24* was like winning the lottery. Traffic to their website, inbound calls, emails, and web forums experienced dramatic increases in traffic."

With the advent of personal media, control is in the hands of the consumer if they choose to accept it. If you are inserting commercial content within the TV program, they can't get around it. Because Canada's broadcasters pick up so much programming from the US, there are fewer opportunities here. Canwest Global recently inserted digitally a Casino Rama logo atop the New York taxi that carried away a fired *Apprentice* candidate. "They can do it in programming simulcast from the US, but this virtual placement was only seen in Canadian markets," suggests Rick Sanderson, general manager, OMD Vancouver.

While onscreen placement has been happening since the 1980s, product placement in print is fairly new and somewhat controversial. The presence of any paid placements would seem troubling for editors who pride themselves on presenting objective news content that supposedly is not influenced by advertisers or other business interests. While being entertained, consumers may seem receptive to product influence, but where editorialized news and reporting is involved, people expect to know what is objective and what has been bought.

Dose, the free daily aimed at the eighteen to thirty-four-year-old market, integrates the three platforms of print, online, and mobile to reach their audience. They sell both ad space and branded/integrated content. The day *Batman Begins* opened in theatres, the entire *Dose* issue was devoted to Batman. The paper boasted seventy editorial integration points, photos, a *Batman* front cover, full-page ads, as well as online and mobile contests and giveaways. Warner Brothers essentially bought the issue. *Dose* called it co-branded. To be fair, advertisers are always looking for publicity and publications for newsworthy content. But the *Dose* example takes the practice to a new level. Dan McLeod, Publisher of the *Georgia Straight*, Vancouver's urban weekly, observes, "Advertisers have become a lot more demanding these days. With three new free dailies, the print competition is very intense, and advertisers feel that this is a good time to demand more, because often they can get it. The commercialization of the daily paper has reached its zenith with the commuter papers. You can actually 'buy' an entire issue of any of them for a price. The *Straight* is one paper that has consistently refused to compromise its editorial integrity by accepting these kinds of ads."

However, some in the advertising community see it differently. "Traditional publications separate advertising and editorial like church and state. I think the twenty-somethings are more accepting. They've grown up in a world of media. They can easily pick it out. As long as it's evident, I don't think they're being fooled," says Rick Anderson, general manager, OMD Vancouver.

And what do consumers think about all this? Pollara recently posed questions for my company on this topic to 1,200 Canadians. In BC, 43% of those surveyed agreed with the statement "Media accept payment to profile a product." Those aged eighteen to thirty-four were the least likely to believe this practice takes place, with 33% agreeing. There was also an education and income effect. The higher the education and the higher the income, the more likely they were to believe paid placement takes place. Although perception may not match reality, relatively low numbers reported that "Seeing a product used on TV or in a movie caused them to view it favourably." In BC only 8% agreed with this statement. However, 18% of those eighteen to twenty-four years of age agreed. And when it comes to "Trusting what is written or reported about a product," 33% of those in BC agreed with the statement. Again youth, those aged eighteen to thirty-four, had the highest trust in editorial and reporting, with 38% agreeing. It appears younger consumers are most influenced by product placement, and those with less education are less likely to question the practice or challenge its influence.

With the media landscape becoming increasingly crowded, product placement is here to stay. And with it come issues of ethics and creative ways to leverage it.

Gauging the Lower Mainland's Appetite for a Daily Dose

■ ■ ■

Business in Vancouver newspaper, May 3, 2005

A note to readers: Since this article was originally published in 2005, there have been significant shifts in Vancouver's print media. *Dose*, the urban daily that was aimed at increasing youth newspaper readership, has since folded its printed product, but remains as an online news and entertainment source. *Metro* and *24 Hours*, other free dailies launched around the same time, continue to battle for reader eyeballs. *24 Hours* shifted from a smaller-format glossy to a tabloid-sized newsprint product. While these newspapers have gained a foothold, paid daily newspaper readership is down. The current economic crisis has taken a toll on print media advertising support. A shift in media consumption habits to online has also had an impact on the readership of many newspapers. Since this is still a story unfolding, I include this piece for reference to show how quickly shifts can take place. And as you can see, I called *Dose's* fate shortly after its launch.

Being a self-confessed print media junkie, I've watched with great interest the latest free daily newspaper battle unfold. Print media relies heavily on the support of readers and advertisers. Marketing is their game. In less than a month Vancouver has been inundated with over three thousand new newspaper boxes and 370,000 copies of new newspapers throughout the Lower Mainland. Three free dailies are now vying for readership in an increasingly crowded newspaper market. Do we really need three new papers? Not likely, but some big-money supporters think there's growth in the "quick read" category aimed primarily at younger readers. Until the battle for eyeballs has been waged, we won't know who will survive.

Why so much interest so quickly? Statistics tell us that readers of paid daily newspapers are aging. The *Vancouver Sun* average reader age is 49 years, the *Province* 45 years, the *Globe* 44.9 years and the *National Post* 45.4 years, while the average age for those living in Greater Vancouver is 45 years. The logic behind the rollout of new free dailies is that if you don't cultivate younger readers, it's bad news for your business model long-term.

These new players feel that existing daily papers are not serving those under forty, or it may just be that they want a piece of the action from alternatives that do reach this market. All three new entrants claim to have created a product that appeals to younger readers, those who are technically savvy, raised in a culture of sound bites and the Internet, used to getting their information and entertainment for free, and aren't interested in longer editorial. Or so goes the focus group feedback.

Let's debunk some of the information surrounding the infusion of new reading material and what it means to you as a reader and as a marketer. First, some facts:

Metro is jointly owned by Canwest (the owners of the *Vancouver Sun* and the *Province*), Torstar and Metro International. *Metro* was started in 1995 and is now the fastest-growing newspaper in the world, with forty-seven *Metro* editions in sixty-nine cities worldwide. They distribute 145,000 copies Monday to Friday in Vancouver, and also have editions in Montreal and

Toronto. Their target is the eighteen to forty-nine-year-old urban commuter seeking an intelligent, quick read. 70% of their readers are under forty-five years of age. The sell: Free, quick-read, relevant news on the go. The edge: First market entry, big-money backers, and an established brand.

24 Hours is jointly owned by Quebecor, a subsidiary of Sun Media Corp and the Jimmy Pattison Group. *24 Hours* was started in 2003 with editions in Toronto and Montreal. They distribute 145,000 copies Monday through Friday in Vancouver and have been at the centre of the controversy over placement of boxes without city permission. Sun Media is the largest chain of tabloids and community newspapers in Canada. Their target is a broad age range of active people with limited time to become informed and entertained. The sell: Free, quick-read tabloid-style journalism made widely available. The edge: Smaller size newsmagazine glossy, established backers, high visibility and publicity.

Dose is owned by Canwest Global. They distribute 80,000 copies Monday to Friday in Vancouver. They have also just launched editions in Calgary, Edmonton, Ottawa, and Toronto. Their target is urban, eighteen to thirty-four years, defined as twenty-something singles and thirty-something couples. *Dose* is a print product which is complemented with an interactive website for forums and peer discussion. The online product has e-commerce capabilities, contesting, email programs, and database marketing capabilities. *Dose's* wireless portal offers such things as movie listings, polls, and games. Concert tickets and MP3 downloads are also available online. The sell: A new-mix multimedia brand for young Canadians, by young Canadians. The edge: Unique approach and content entrusted with talented youth to reach their peers.

In Toronto and Montreal, free commuter dailies have gained a substantial number of readers at the expense of some traditional newspapers, NADbank readership figures show. However, NADbank also shows that overall newspaper readership across the country remained stable between 2003 and 2004. It is questionable whether new free dailies will actually pick up a substantial new market of younger readers, with the possible exception of *Dose*, which seems to be squaring off with the *Georgia Straight*. Time will tell if their innovative print and electronic vehicle will cultivate a loyal following. If Canwest can resist the temptation to send in someone over fifty to fix it if it doesn't deliver good quarterly results, it may well find a youthful niche. Early return rates are reportedly as high as 75% for *Metro*. They do not have an exclusive transit distribution agreement here as they do with the TTC in Toronto, so they are relying on surface street commuters for pickup. Return rates for *24 Hours* were not available, but as long as there is a battle over distribution boxes their pickup numbers will be in flux.

Over the coming months the new free dailies will be battling for the hearts and minds of readers and advertisers. Market leaders are not easily dislodged, and it takes time to carve out a new niche. My projection? *Dose* will be toast within two years. *Metro* will remain if it gets support of national advertising campaigns in multiple Canadian markets. *24 Hours* will emerge as the strongest product and get the greatest support from the local market.

An update on ownership: Jimmy Pattison disposed of his interest in *24 Hours* in 2007. It is now owned by Sun Media, a Quebecor Media Company. *Metro* newspaper is currently owned by Metro International and Torstar Corporation.

Marketing to Women

■ ■ ■

This is a topic I write and speak about extensively. For so long marketers seemed to ignore women or miss the mark in their communications with close to half the population. There's still appalling stuff out there, aimed only at men. I experience it daily, but we're starting to see some changes in this area, and not surprisingly, according to my research, the changes are positively affecting sales with men too.

But perhaps the single biggest trend that marketers appear poised to miss is the influence of baby boomer women. I'm constantly amazed at the malaise there seems to be around this topic. Perhaps that's because targeting a woman over fifty was seldom ever done in the past, and it was seen to lack sizzle or opportunity. Perhaps it's because marketing departments often are primarily run by those under fifty. Or perhaps it's because a young thirty-year-old guy can't write good copy that appeals to older women. Whatever the reason, the companies who get it right are going to mine gold. Trust me on this one.

Nintendo Wii Fit
Targets the CHO

• • •

Business in Vancouver newspaper, July 1, 2008

From a marketing perspective, what do teen boys in basements with computer game consoles in pursuit of fast-paced action heroes and unattainable women have in common with thirty-five-year-old and older Moms? Conventional wisdom would say, not much. But a departure from conventional tactics is exactly what Nintendo has done with the incredibly successful Wii, and the recent May 21 launch of Wii Fit. Aiming square at the CHO (Chief Household Officer), known as Mom, Nintendo did what most gaming companies dared not do - develop and market a product to an entirely new audience, one traditionally pretty skeptical of the category.

Video gaming changed dramatically when Nintendo launched Wii. Billed as a social gaming experience, Wii combined motion-sensing technology in a remote control with on-screen interactivity. It was simple, affordable, and had broad appeal. "Our vision was to create games for people six through ninety-five years old. We wanted to appeal to different groups and get more people playing," says Ron Bertram, GM, Nintendo Canada.

While the Wii was targeted at Mom making buying decisions for her family, the Wii Fit is clearly aimed at engaging her directly. The Wii Fit puts the whole body through a focused workout using a pressure sensitive board to control motion, direction, and action used in yoga, balance games, aerobics, and strength training. The company devoted extensive resources to supervised in store, mall, trade show, and cinema sampling; seeded online discussions, word of mouth, as well as traditional media promotion all aimed at the thirty-five-plus woman. It's quite the departure from the battlefields that Microsoft and Sony occupy seeking out that illusive young male. While Nintendo is not about to abandon traditional markets of success with other product lines, their new segment strategy is an interesting departure. So how did they engage Mom and more importantly, why did they bother?

"We realized there was a problem in the gaming industry. The number of people playing was decreasing. We wanted to expand the market and reach people who weren't playing, which was 60% of families, including those thirty-five-plus women. We realized that women were the most influential in all those groups," notes Matt Ryan, media communications, Nintendo Canada. Consumer research indicates that women control 85% of household spending. Mom not only controls how the money is spent, but how the family spends recreation time. It was a natural match for reaching an expanded market. No other competitor was playing in that field. In marketing terms, that's called an opportunity.

Nintendo knew that there were perceived barriers to gaming. Women saw it as antisocial, intimidating, and often violent. The answer? Create a product that was social, simple to use, fun, and could engage the whole family. With Wii, a simple-to-use, gracefully designed motion-sensing remote replaced the traditional massive game console, software installation, and excessive buttons and commands. The Wii Fit utilizes a motion-sensitive balance board. Over forty activities in the areas of yoga, aerobics, strength, and balance offer a diversity that appeals to everyone, while firmly engaging Mom directly by combining fun and fitness. "Mom is really the gateway to reaching a broad market. She's a key influencer on others," says Matt Ryan.

Clearly Nintendo has tapped key marketing-to-women insights with its launch of Wii Fit:

1. Simplicity is important. They've made their product simple to use and understand.

2. Women love technology that simplifies their life, they don't just love technology. This is technology with purpose. It brings the family together. It's social and involves active entertainment. Or it can simply be a way for her to work out at home.

3. Women crave an escape. Wii Fit offers an escape to the yoga studio, the ski slopes, or some one-on-one time with a personal trainer. All in the comforts of home.

4. Respect her time and don't question or compete with her stress. Can't make it to the gym? Baby sleeping? No problem, the gym is now in your home. Set-up is simple. No techno genius required. No frustration. No wasted time.

5. Aesthetics are important. Wii Fit has one simple white mat with clean lines. You'd think Apple had designed it.

6. Women talk and have concentric circles of influence. Nintendo is actively harnessing the power of word of mouth with an emphasis on experiential marketing through product trial. They want women to understand the product so they will talk about it and change the stigmas around gaming. This power of word of mouth is exponential.

With Wii sales topping 7.4 million units in 2007, it seems a long way from that dark basement Nintendo's competitors are playing in.

Did Lululemon's Mansy Joke Miss the Marketing Mark?

. . .

Marketing magazine, April 28, 2008

"We just wanted to have some fun. We don't take ourselves too seriously," said Sarah Gardiner, communications manager for Lululemon, regarding their recent ad featuring the "mansy." On April 1st, the day the mansy was promised to arrive in limited quantities, Lululemon fessed up to an April Fool's Day joke.

In case you missed it, the full-page ad featured a buff male striking a yoga pose on Vancouver's Kits Beach wearing the mansy, a clingy one-piece featuring a high cut leg and thong for men. It ran in urban weeklies across Canada and the US. The small type on the ad explained the mansy would be available in limited quantities on April 1st. That, along with their communications people refusing to comment on the ad when it first ran, was a pretty good indication that it was a stunt. An April Fools' joke. Good one, Lululemon, or was it?

My initial response to the ad: A Lululemon full-page ad? They never do full-page print ads. This was different. Someone new must have been handling the advertising. I really wish I hadn't seen that. Nice buff body, but not even that could save him from the visual tragedy and the reason why women never want their man to wear a Speedo. Too much information on the high leg cut. Maybe it was a subtly targeted at the gay community? It was available April 1st. It must be a joke. But even if it was a joke, why would they be doing this? Was it to generate talk and free publicity? Even if was a joke and a publicity stunt, how would it speak to the target group? It seemed to be male-centred humour, not female. Their product line split indicates a strong female skew. Women would look at this and say, what were they thinking? Oh my God, maybe it wasn't a joke. I might actually see a guy wearing it. Why am I feeling uncomfortable? This ad was a huge a departure from their core message and who their target is.

My initial conclusion was that someone new must be doing the advertising. They did it for free and made it cutting edge so they could prove how they could generate publicity and talk. Plus, they wanted to enter it in an awards show. Male creative directors would love it and shower them in awards. There would be a lot of backslapping and jokes about how brilliant it was. The women in the room, and a large part of the target group, should Lululemon actually care about how advertising drives sales, would scratch their heads and wonder what happened to the brand that they thought they had an emotional connection with.

Was it irreverent and in keeping with the company's culture or did it show a disconnect with the predominantly female customer base? Advertising executives in Vancouver, where Lululemon has their head office, gave it a mixed review. The day the ad broke, Andeen Pitt, VP, media and business development, Wasserman and Partners Advertising, said, "I can't believe it's not real. Why else would they take such a risk?" Victoria Gray, general manager, Taxi West, remarked, "I'm curious to hear what the follow-up on this is. I totally agree with your conclusions." Once the news was out, Gray commented, "What was the point? I'm kind of stunned. How does that make us feel, as their target group, more affinity towards the brand? What does it gain them?" Admittedly this analysis may be too deep for something that was created in - house and done for fun. But it does call us to consider how all messaging should be true to a brand and its target group.

And for those women breathing a sigh of relief that they won't hazard a chance encounter with a mansy-clad guy anytime soon, the assurance may be premature. "We've had phone calls and people coming into the store wanting to buy it," says Gardiner. "We are a company that responds to customer feedback. If we see enough interest, we may have to produce it." Only in Vancouver.

The Power of Baby Boomer Women

■ ■ ■

Business in Vancouver newspaper, January 8, 2007

Since baby boomers first burst on the scene in the early sixties as young adults, they have been the darling of the business and the advertising industry, based on the sheer economic opportunity of meeting the needs of such a huge group. Baby boomers, born 1946 to 1964, will be aged forty-three to sixty-two years old this year. Every seven seconds in Canada, someone turns fifty. But something curious seems to be happening. Just when this powerhouse group has reached the peak of their earning years, with elevated disposable income and the health to enjoy it for many years to come, they are being dropped for a more youthful model. Call it the ultimate middle-aged affair, and nowhere is this more apparent than in marketers' approach to female baby boomers.

Today's woman over fifty is an empowered and self-sufficient economic powerhouse. She has become more assertive with age, is increasingly free from old responsibilities, and is eager to embrace new adventures. She belongs to the first generation of working women. Those over fifty make up 27% of the population, yet control 70% of the wealth. She stands to inherit even more wealth from her parents, and is highly likely to outlive her spouse. Couple this with the fact that women buy or influence 85% or more of what is sold, and she should definitely be on a marketer's radar screen.

Yet in a world of size twos, celebrity endorsements, and super-sized cheap food, it appears this is definitely not the case. Whether it's failure to understand the sheer enormity of the opportunity or an infatuation with all things new and youthful, many businesses don't get women over fifty.

Oh sure, there's the easy stuff, which we're starting to see, like readable type sizes, better lighting, smaller healthy portions, and consideration to product design and service options for this group. These apply to both men and women. To really connect with boomer women, businesses have to harness the nuances to understand what is important.

1. Authenticity and honesty are critical. Women portrayed in ads need to be realistic, not ideal. That's why celebrity endorsements fall flat with this group. Boomer women are drawn to people they feel are like them. Authentic, by all means attractive, but some flaws are just fine. This is why the Dove campaign for real beauty has struck such a chord with this group. It used real women, flaws and all, in an industry rife with impossible-to-achieve ideals.

2. Social strategy is very important. Good corporate citizenship matters. But this social strategy needs to be at the heart and soul of a business, not applied like philanthropic lipstick at the end. There is a shift from focus on oneself to a focus on others at this age. This is particularly evident with women. According to a recent Pollara poll of 1,200 Canadians, 84% of fifty-year-old women felt it was important to deal with businesses that make the world a better place through their actions, while 73% of men of this age felt the same. Additionally, 62% of fifty-year-old women said an ad that demonstrates social responsibility resonates with them, while 48% of men of this age felt the same. 81% of women over fifty agree that the time has come to deal with environmental sustainability, while 69% of men the same age agreed. "Women tend to be more passionate about social strategy and become more so as they get older, wereas men tend to stay the same as they age," suggests Michael Antecol, VP, Pollara. There is a social movement building, and boomer women are at the forefront.

3. Relationship building and storytelling matter. Women value relationships, and boomer women in particular enjoy the camaraderie and company of those like them. This network has powerful word-of-mouth ability. The surging popularity of book clubs is a great illustration of relationship building. "Sociologically speaking, this is part of how we root ourselves in a community - by creating interconnected webs of relationships and by making alliances with others of like mind, something women tend to be particularly adept at," notes Elinor Morris, manager and book club founder for the Book Warehouse. Recently, the North Vancouver Recreation Commission published a recreation guide targeted at baby boomer adults. Titled *Live Your Best Life*, it is an attractive adult guide to active healthy living. Beyond the fitness schedules and programming information, it is the "stories of people just like you" interwoven throughout which make it effective at reaching boomer women.

Baby boomer women are vibrantly independent and part of a vibrant set of peers. Think ageless, healthy, and authentic. Think relationships and social responsibility. Think of the opportunities.

Reaching Men through Marketing to Women

• • •

Business in Vancouver newspaper, March 7, 2006

Just when you thought the gender mix thing was becoming balanced, a marketer tosses this statistic at you - women buy or influence the purchase of 85% or more of what is sold. If this seems a little unfair to you, consider just how unsatisfied this powerful consumer group is with many industries. A recent Canadian survey by the Thomas Yaccato Group revealed these women's satisfaction levels: Supermarkets/grocery stores - 76%; Cosmetic companies - 56%; Hotels - 54%; Home electronics - 51%. And those that didn't even make passing grades? Banks - 33%; Telephone companies - 46%; Computer companies - 36%; Airlines - 33%; Car dealers - 27%.

As customers, we know that being 50% satisfied is far from a pass. It's a desperate failure. And it becomes even more a mark of failure when you consider this: when you satisfy female consumers, you will likely exceed the expectations of your male customers. Call them tough, call them discerning, but if you pay attention to what women want, you'll achieve increased sales success overall. Canadian Tire and Home Depot, long the domains of men, tools, and hardware, have both taken an interest in reaching women recently. Canadian Tire opened a new 63,000 square foot store in Vancouver last year. The design, named Concept 20/20 because it has 20% more floor space than traditional stores, features hardwood floors and decorating boutiques with a real emphasis on home décor. The format change was made to help the chain appeal to women. And it has resulted in higher average sales per transaction. Where sales used to be 30% to women in traditional stores, they have now climbed to 50%. Home Depot launched their "Dream Book" catalogue to focus on inspirational living spaces and how to create them. Their advertising has become female friendly and appears in design-inspired magazines. Their website features both an empowered do-it-yourself man and a woman prominently on the home page. And once you enter the site, you are greeted with designer home décor photos and the message "Decorate with style. Great deals on what you need to transform any room into a sanctuary." Contrast the new Home Depot to the traditional big-box format. Their new stores feature a design sensitive layout with fewer rows of product and more home décor design areas. Since Home Depot made the changes, female shoppers account for 50% of transactions, and overall sales have increased 6.1%. The business of satisfying female consumers is a complex issue, but here is a summary of what some businesses are doing to make a difference. When you address these issues, you not only satisfy women, you also sell more to men.

1. Eliminate anything causing stress when dealing with your business. This often includes time-wasting activities. Lack of attentive service, unnecessary lineups, unknowledgeable novice sales staff, undelivered promises, wasted time, undependable products, complex assembly or product instructions, missing pieces, and complicated policies or processes are some of the worst offenders.

2. When people shop with kids in tow there is a need for ease and a need for speed. Businesses need to reduce or eliminate

stress inducers and introduce stress relievers. Eliminate waiting, lineups, breakables, and sugary food at the two-foot level. These require management and more energy. Do add services such as delivery, assembly, quick checkout, child minding or entertainment, clean and accessible washrooms, and nutritious cheap food. The necessity for food or washrooms while shopping with young kids has robbed many businesses of would-be sales.

3. Keep things simple. Give customers what they want, not what you can design or think they need. Consumer electronics and telecommunications are big offenders in this area.

4. Understand that men and women reach a buying decision in different ways, and often communicate their readiness to buy differently too. Women tend to gather research from a number of sources - friends, experts, the Internet, magazines, consumer reports, and the media. Men tend to eliminate unnecessary data to reach an objective decision. It's not about which method is better, it's about respecting the differences.

5. Word of mouth is powerful, but make sure customers have a reason to like you.

6. Aesthetics are important. Design and service matter. The design and layout of the store, the consistency in messaging and promotional materials, the attitudes of salespeople, the knowledge level and efficiency of staff, and cleanliness of the washrooms are all important details.

7. Be consistent in your marketing mix. All communications must be integrated. If a customer walks into your store and the experience doesn't live up to the marketing, you have failed.

If You're Not Marketing to Women, You're Missing a Big Part of the Market

■ ■ ■

Business in Vancouver newspaper, July 26, 2005

We know that men and women's minds are wired differently. This realization may have come courtesy of a pricey psychologist or an insightful friend following a crash and burn in the romance department. But a funny thing happened on the way to the shrink. Business got in on the action. Many companies have finally realized that a failed romance with 50% of their potential customer base, and in most cases a whole lot more, has been costing them money. So started the courtship of the female consumer and the recent interest in marketing to women.

Relationship parallels aside, why should you care? Because women buy or influence the purchase of 85% or more of what is sold. Clearly, they are a powerful consumer group. A recent Canadian study by the Thomas Yaccato Group revealed that all industries other than food and supermarkets fell well below the 80% satisfaction level with women consumers. In fact, most industries came in well under 60%. And the influence of women on purchases goes way beyond clothes, furniture, and cosmetics. This influence is across the board. It's time to listen up. In short, here are the ten points you need to know:

1. Don't question or compete with women's stress, just accept it. Do not increase her stress level by irritating her more with poor service, unnecessary lineups, or complicated return policies. Stressed people are lousy shoppers. They frequently share their ill humour.

2. Consider the needs of women with children. Shopping with kids in tow can be difficult, but it is a reality for many. Learn how to make their lives a little easier.

3. Reduce or eliminate time-wasting activities. Through her stressed eyes, she has no time to spare. If your product or service promises to simplify her life, make sure it actually does.

4. Simplicity is important. Make your offer simple to understand and simple to use. If complexity robs her of time, the stress level goes up. Refer back to point #1.

5. Understand that for women, decision-making takes time. It's informed and deliberate. Tell the truth and respect the desire to assimilate the data. Women integrate information and experiences to make decisions. This usually takes time. Men eliminate unnecessary details so an informed objective decision can be reached. This process can be seen as fast, and efficient. It's not about which is right, it's about respecting the differences.

6. Women talk. You want them to talk about you in a positive light. This can be a source of your best or your worst advertising. You have little control once the word is out, so make sure you give her something positive to talk about.

7. When women shop, they see everything. Aesthetics, design, and service matter. Present your product or service in a way that matches her decision process. Help her envision the completed project. Exceptional service will make an impression. Refer back to point six.

8. Women love technology that simplifies their life. They

don't just love technology. You need to understand the difference. Are software, phone, cable, and Internet service providers listening? You should be. Research indicates that women make or influence the majority of these product decisions.

9. Understand that women crave an escape. If you can position your business to deliver comfort, a reward, or a real benefit, women will notice and appreciate it. There is a reason why spas and coffee shops are so popular. They offer a mini holiday from the stress and mundane of everyday life.

10. Be consistent in your marketing mix and make sure all elements of communication are integrated. Inconsistencies will make her question your sincerity. Don't think she won't notice. She will, and she'll likely talk. Refer back to point six.

"If you meet the needs of female consumers, you will exceed the expectations of men," says Yaccato. So this is not all about increasing your sales to women; it's about increasing your sales - period. Think of women as a business barometer. To be successful you need to approach both genders with intelligent marketing. It's not about making it appeal to women; it's about doing everything so that fundamentally you are taking women seriously.

I recently worked with 2C Visual Communications, a film production company, and hit the streets of Vancouver to do a little research of my own as part of a documentary on marketing to women. We interviewed leaders in the advertising industry, businesses who are doing it right, as well as countless women on the streets of Vancouver. I've incorporated much of what we learned into this article.

Just Ask a Woman, by Mary Lou Quinlan, of New York, and *The 80% Minority*, by Joanne Thomas Yaccato, of Toronto, are two excellent sources of information on this subject.

Savvy Marketers Know How to Sell to Women

■ ■ ■

Business in Vancouver newspaper, January 11, 2005

It's the new year and you're no doubt reflecting on some of the decisions you made in December. Does the world really look better on a new flat-screen TV? Did the kids really need all that plastic? And speaking of plastic, just what happened to your credit card anyway? Buyer's remorse meets income reality. Add these seasonal factors to an already collectively stressed population, and it becomes nasty territory for a marketer to navigate. Women in particular view themselves as a stressed lot. Statistics Canada reports that one-third of married women employed full-time with children at home reported high levels of stress. Women in the sandwich generation caring for children and aging parents report spending twice as much time on these activities compared to men. And working women without kids, still report higher levels of stress than working men without kids. Even those under twenty-five, including high school kids reported fairly high levels of stress, with young women being twice as likely as young men to be severely time stressed.

Why should you care about the stressed-out female consumer? Because women buy or influence the purchase of 85% or more of what is sold. They are a powerful group. And in addition to the stresses that women feel are thrust upon them, they tend to be masters of self-induced stress. As marketers, you need to understand what that means to your business. Here's what you need to know:

1. Don't question or compete with her stress. Accept it. You can-not effectively connect with female consumers if stress is in the way. No connection, no sale. If your product or service contributes to her stress because it is undependable, complicated, or requires unavailable time on her part, she will go to a competitor. Are your assembly or product use instructions complex or missing? Do you have phone advice readily available with no waiting? If there is a problem, are your salespeople knowledgeable and empowered to handle it promptly? The last thing you want to do is create more stress. Remember, not all women love to shop. It's a task that needs doing for many.

2. Consider the needs of stressed-out women with kids. If you become a burden, she will shut you out. Shopping with kids in tow is a reality for many women. Do you have a public washroom available? If she has to leave your store she likely won't be back. Is your business kid friendly? Play areas for kids while women shop for clothes can turn a "bolt and buy" mission into a more pleasurable shopping experience. Hint: this likely means she'll spend more money. Is your business a minefield waiting for a toddler's attack? Low-lying breakables, gadgets, and sugary food items may be desirable for the kids, but will require management and energy just to navigate your store. Mom won't be coming back. Shell's "Speed Pass" pay-at-the-pump key chain is brilliant. It saves time and caters to moms. The kids stay in the car, and a purchase is quick and easy.

3. Look at your product or service through stressed eyes. Focus on the reality of her life, not your version of it. You need to solve her problems. Save her time and keep it simple. Make any stress associated with dealing with you, your product or service disappear. A complicated return procedure wastes time. Lineups at checkout waste time. Not being able to find something quickly or not getting knowledgeable advice complicates matters. And if you have to make her wait, do it with caution. Try pressing *555 next time you're on hold with Westjet. "It doesn't do anything, but it makes you feel better," you'll be cheerfully informed later. What it does do is make you laugh. And during that time, they have bought a minute of your time graciously. Mr. Lube gives customers coffee and a paper in their car while getting their oil changed. They have recognized that the wait time can actually be turned into break time. Stress meets opportunity. It doesn't cost them much and it works. What could you do to turn a visit to your business into a short escape?

4. Simplify your product or service. Just because it's easier for you to do something one way, doesn't make it the best way for your customer. Look at all processes in your business through the customer's eyes. What is involved to return something? Just because you can invent a new product feature doesn't mean consumers will want it. Let's hope software and electronics manufacturers are listening. Step back and assess. Will it require time to learn how to use or install it? Is the benefit worth the effort?

A savvy marketer makes a customer's stress go away by anticipating their needs, respecting their time, exceeding their expectations, and connecting with them on an emotional level. If you think like your customer, they will have reason to be loyal to you. And by addressing what stresses out women and reducing that stress, I guarantee you'll sell a whole lot more to men too.

Navigating to
Venus and Mars

■ ■ ■

Business in Vancouver newspaper, March 9, 2004

Could it be that marketers are finally figuring out the Mars-Venus thing? For years the differences in men and women's behaviour toward buying products and services has been largely ignored. Why should you care? Because, as noted before, women buy or influence the purchase of 85% or more of what is sold. Clearly they are a powerful consumer group. That means that even if you are not in an industry such as beauty, health, fashion, food, or family products, that have typically grasped the importance of the female decision-maker-you need to pay attention. What makes this shift in interest important is the trend by typically male-dominated industries to recognize the power of the female customer and incorporate changes to welcome her.

Home improvement is a huge consumer sector. Estimated at $31 billion a year in Canada, it is dominated by chain retailers such as Home Depot, Rona, Home Hardware, and Ikea. With knowledge that women have a hand in 75% of all home improvement decisions, these stores are making a number of changes to appeal to the female consumer. Home Depot has been known as a tool mecca for males, with shelves and shelves of product by category. They are now orienting one side of store inventory more toward women. They have grouped home décor items and merchandise displays to help consumers envision a completed project. Home Depot has branched out, offering flooring and kitchen installation, services of particular interest to female consumers. But since do-it-yourself is still their focus, they have designed a number of in-store clinics for women only. Their website seems to be designed with the female in mind, showcasing gifts and design accessories, and offering a number of renovation tips. Featuring women as prominently as men, new advertising portrays empowered women using power tools to complete projects on their own. The tag line, "You can do it. We can help," positions Home Depot as the source for the do-it-yourself man or woman.

What could be more intimidating than the prospect of a consumer electronics purchase? While price-sensitive retailers such as Future Shop still don't seem to get it, some high-end electronics retailers are making inroads with women. Audio and home theatre has traditionally been a male-dominated industry. However, retailers such as Sound Plus have long understood the influence of women on purchase decisions. Although the store traffic is skewed male, Doug Argue, president of Sound Plus, estimates that women influence up to 80% of purchases ultimately made in the store. Several years ago they renovated extensively to devote the entire upstairs to demonstration rooms designed to help customers envision the product in their own home. "A lot of guys will get jazzed up about the capabilities of the technology and how it will advance their status and power, but women typically want to know how it will enhance their lifestyle. Reliability, beauty, ease of use, and how it will work in the whole design of the home are major concerns," says Mark Blackwood of Sound Plus's custom division. Carol Campbell, publisher of *The Connected Guide to the Digital Home* is more blunt in her assessment. "Men are in love with the technology itself. Women take technologies and turn them into appliances. They strip even the fanciest gizmo of jargon and all that is mysterious to determine its usefulness." Sound Plus has acknowledged the different ways that women approach home theatre and audio systems, and how these differences affect buying behaviour. They train their sales staff to position the product appropriately for the male or female consumer.

In a world where 81% of all products, both business and consumer, are purchased by women, there's a good chance your business could benefit by considering the needs of this influential demographic. Here's what you need to know to sell to her:

1. She's stressed, so respect her time, and if your product or service promises to simplify her life, make sure it does.

2. Keep it simple. Make it simple to understand and simple to use. If complexity robs her of precious spare minutes, the stress level goes up and your product or service will be on the way out.

3. Present your product or service in a way that matches her decision process. Help her envision the completed project. Extra effort on her part takes time. More time adds stress. You may see a pattern emerging here!

4. Be consistent in your marketing mix and make sure all elements of communication are integrated. Inconsistencies will make her question your sincerity.

5. Give her the information she wants. Tell the truth, and respect her desire to assimilate the data before making a buying decision. This may take time. Then when she's ready to buy, make it easy and stress free.

Of course, several of these points could apply to male consumers too, so it just makes good business sense to consider them as well in your marketing efforts.

A note to readers: Sound Plus was acquired by La Scala Home Cinema + Integrated Media in 2009 after a change in management.

Advertising and Public Relations

. . .

Publicity is free coverage. Advertising is paid coverage. This chapter looks at both of these methods to get your message out there. Getting publicity and media coverage is a lot of hard work. Sometimes all the hard work doesn't even amount to coverage, which can make it even more disappointing. Consistency seems to be key. You need to be seeking publicity all the time. Creativity and original ideas will give you a whole lot more material to mine. And a good publicist can make your life a lot easier. Media convergence has also made publicity efforts more challenging. There are fewer independents to target, and editorial decision-making is in the hands of an increasingly smaller, yet powerful group. This has made having a strong relationship with the media even more important.

The media is now much more willing to cross the lines between advertising and editorial than it used to be. And since youth seem open to this approach and confident in their ability to objectively view information, this trend is likely to continue. Although from a purely objective readership standpoint this approach could be questioned, it does offer some opportunities for creative marketers. Online user-generated content also puts an interesting spin on this topic, where the world of bloggers and users becomes increasingly important. We have increasingly seen the use of seeded publicity stunts online as a huge growth area.

The other challenging area for marketers is the increasingly fragmented area of paid advertising. Although traditional mass-market vehicles such as outdoor, print, radio, and TV are still very powerful, they are becoming less so as major shifts take place in consumer behaviour. Balance seems to be the key here as integrated marketing communications become increasingly important. Successful companies are utilizing a mix of paid multimedia, free publicity, and new electronic media (known as Web 2.0) customer engagement.

Creating Media Buzz About Business Can Pay Dividends

■ ■ ■

Business in Vancouver newspaper, December 19, 2006

It seems these days we are inundated with advertising at every turn. Companies spend more and more on marketing, and we pay less and less attention as competition for our interest elevates. So how do you get better results from your marketing? You get people to talk about your stuff. You generate word of mouth. You get free publicity in the media. You get buzz. Generating positive word of mouth can be one of the single most effective marketing tools you have at your disposal. Because word of mouth and generating media coverage comes via a third party, it is seen as authentic. It tends to get remembered and it's free. What could possibly be better?

Although it is the least expensive form of advertising, it is also the most time consuming. And because you can't buy it, you have little control over the accuracy of what is said or written. To get publicity you must have the imagination to produce newsworthy content and publicize it. You must have influential media contacts to offer news to, and you need to nurture these contacts and keep them current. And finally, you must have the persistence to follow things through in order to get the news coverage you are looking for. So how do you get news? How do you create buzz? Here are some ideas.

1. Announce something new about your business.
2. Explain something unique or unusual about your business.
3. Announce an upcoming event.
4. Connect your offering to what's in the news right now.
5. Give survey results.
6. Leverage a holiday or special event.
7. Connect your business to a current trend.
8. Make a controversial claim (and be able to back it up!).
9. Make a humorous announcement.
10. Stage an event.

■ ■ ■

You will need to put together a press kit for the media. It should include:
1. Your one-page release
2. A short note about why you're sending the press kit.
3. Photo with caption.
4. An attractive folder to hold everything.
5. A one-sheet brief about your company and background.
6. Your business card and contact information.
As we move increasingly into an electronic age, email press releases are becoming much more common and desired. If you write a tight press release you may even find media picking it up almost directly. Seems editors like that cut-and-paste function! But remember, if you're sending a press release by email, put the release within the content of the email, not as an attachment. Unsolicited attachments are less likely to be opened and may be feared to contain viruses. Make your subject heading catchy and avoid words or phrases used in spam, which may cause your message to be filtered out.

If you are fortunate enough to be interviewed, you need to be prepared.

1. Practise. Better yet, get coaching.
2. Know what makes you or your business different.
3. Practise communicating your message.
4. Identify three main points, and always bring questions back to these points.

One local business that has harnessed the power of capturing media and creating buzz is Executive Search Dating. They bill themselves as the "Dating Headhunters," and their services are aimed at busy professionals. While matching agents interview clients to create a profile, the "Cupid Strike Force" patrols events throughout the city proactively searching for the perfect match. Thorough screening and all dating arrangements as well as follow-up and refinement of matches make for an appealing package for busy attractive professional singles. After having limited success with traditional paid advertising, company founder and president Paddi Rice embarked on extensive efforts to create word of mouth and buzz about his company's services.

One stunt saw them place valuables such as Rolex watches and luxury car keys in bear traps at strategic places in Vancouver's financial district. Signs exclaiming "Leave the hunting to us" were placed close by. The guerrilla campaign, the brain-child of Rethink, a Vancouver marketing firm, garnered them coverage in *Metro* and *Marketing Magazine*. By using their "Cupid Strike Force" to interview people about dating in Vancouver, they have been able to generate their own research, which has helped them get coverage with CBC AM, News 1130AM, and The Beat 94.5FM *The Beat*, the *Vancouver Sun*, the *Globe and Mail*, *Business in Vancouver*, *Global TV*, and *A Channel*. The Beat featured a promotion called "Shred your X" where they set up a paper shredder on a busy downtown street at lunchtime. Listeners were invited to shred photos and letters in exchange for a first date with Executive Search Dating.

Paddi Rice explains that there are two important aspects to media. The first is getting it regularly to keep a presence out there. The second is making sure people see their media. The company actively promotes all coverage received on their website. Rice also recognized the benefits of professional media coaching, which he received from Optimedia. He interviews well.

Harnessing buzz is hard work. But getting people to talk about your stuff is worth it. And as the media universe gets increasingly cluttered, it's an authentic way to cut through and be heard.

Are You Really Ready to Advertise?

■ ■ ■

Business in Vancouver newspaper, January 13, 2004

Let's suppose you have some concerns about your business. Things seem to be running smoothly, but sales growth is flat. You know a good way to grow your customer base is to advertise. Consider this for a moment. For what it will cost you to place a full-page ad in the *Georgia Straight*, you could send an undergrad arts and science honours student to UBC for an entire year. (Approximately $4,000.) You could fund an entire four-year degree at UBC for the cost of a full-page ad in Saturday's *Vancouver Sun*. Want to produce and buy a prime-time television campaign for a thirty-second commercial? Prepare to part with some serious cash. The point is, advertising is not cheap. Like a good education, it's a wise investment, which will reap rewards if done right. Choose the right media, reach the right target group, deliver the right message, and you'll strike gold. A poor message, or worse, no real message, delivered in the wrong media missing your target audience is money squandered. But before you purchase advertising, you must assess your business and your marketing plan. Are you really ready to advertise?

Advertising types can dazzle you with a situation analysis, objectives, creative briefs, strategies, and media plans, but it fundamentally boils down to this: are you doing anything worth bragging about?

If you aren't, you don't have an advertising problem. You have a marketing problem. Don't spend a dime on advertising until you have your business in order. Here are some questions to ask yourself:

1. Are you delivering compelling functional, emotional, and financial value to your customers? Your product or service must be functionally superior to your competitor's. If your business creates a strong connection with the customer, making customers feel valued, good about themselves, or happy that your business solved a problem for them, you have connected at an emotional level. You must also deliver the perception of good value by offering the best price, or by making them believe the price they paid is a fair exchange for a superior product or service. If you can't clearly define your functional, emotional, and financial value to customers, you're not ready to advertise.

2. Are your target customers well understood? You must know their demographic profile, their values, and their preferences. If you don't know who your target customers are, what they really value, and what your compelling value is to them, you're not ready to advertise.

3. Can you honestly say you're really good at what you do? Does your business differentiate itself from your competitors in a meaningful way? Do you always think of your customers first? Get good, then advertise. You must know and be able to identify to your customers what makes you different from your competitors. Every single pricing decision, display, design, and operational system must be designed with customer interaction top of mind. Why would you want to bring in new customers if they weren't going to have an excellent experience? You want them to love you and spread the word. Which brings us to the next point...

4. Your most cost-effective and powerful advertising is not purchased. It is earned. The enthusiastic recommendation of satisfied customers is far more effective than any advertising campaign you can buy. With a plethora of the mundane at their doorstep, consumers are thirsty for a find, something worth seeking out, something that delivers a superior experience, unparalleled value, something worth bragging about. You want these customers to be recommending you! When the experience you deliver is so compelling that every new customer your advertising attracts enthusiastically recommends you to others, you have achieved leverage. Don't buy advertising until you know you've got leverage.

5. Does your planned advertising present you as the media or respected authorities view you? Advertising is only effective if what you say about yourself is consistent with what others are saying about you. If you claim you give the best service or price, but they say you don't, your advertising will be largely wasted. You need to create a consistent and honest identity before you advertise.

6. And remember, customers aren't stupid, so don't lie. If you aren't the cheapest, the best, the largest, the quickest, the most exclusive, or the most preferred, don't tell them you are! Air Canada needn't tell us about good customer service. They should show us. Unless you can stake a genuine claim in this area, avoid false statements. You'll risk losing leverage with customers forever once they've had an experience that doesn't substantiate your claim.

So, are you really ready to spend big money on advertising, or do you have some work to do first? Advertising is a good investment, but choose to do it wisely, after all your research is done.

Good Advertising Means Knowing Your Target and Choosing Your Medium

■ ■ ■

Business in Vancouver newspaper, July 27, 2004

Have you heard or seen any good ads lately? Working in the marketing and advertising industry, my view of media has been forever tainted by looking at the ads first. This insatiable appetite for a creative approach to selling through clever messages and media choices causes me to constantly evaluate the advertising we see around us. Good ads drive sales, not just win awards; and good ads don't have to be expensive, just well targeted. Advertising that creates mind-share means very little. Mind-share still must be transferred into something tangible. Market share is all that really matters because it affects sales. I'm a fan of good creative, but only if it makes the cash register sing. So what makes for great advertising? Let's look at the fundamentals.

1. The target market must be well defined.

2. You must understand explicitly the mindset of your target group: what motivates them, their values, attributes, and characteristics.

3. You must have defined objectives and a desired outcome for the campaign. These usually include, among other things, an increase in sales.

4. Your message must resonate with your target audience, through the content and information conveyed and the creative chosen.

5. The media vehicles selected must deliver your target group and suit the campaign. Sounds like Advertising 101, right? Then why do many businesses get it wrong?

Direct mail can be a very effective vehicle, but here's an example of a piece that missed its target miserably. I recently received a package from the Perfect Pen and Stationery Company. They had printed a pen with my company name on it, prefaced with the words "I stole this from…" The letter kindly suggested I might like to buy hundreds of these things to give to my clients. Now, why would I want to give my client a gift, a tacky one at that, with a message that effectively turns them into a thief? Is this a brand identity I want to create? Just what were they thinking? Perhaps I wasn't their target group. But then why did I receive the mailing? At the very least they misunderstood my values and what would motivate me to buy.

The series of Telus TV spots and print creative using cute animals, white space and a catchy soundtrack and message to promote the company's technology are right on target. The campaign objective is clear, the message resonates with the audience, the media vehicles are well chosen for the target group, and the creative taps into the mindset and values of the target audience in a clever way. The spots are brilliant. And they almost make me forget any problem I've ever had with Telus!

But sometimes what seems like brilliant creative can miss the mark completely when it comes to driving sales. An example of advertising creative which got a lot of buzz was a TV spot for Miller Lite beer. It featured two women dining at a café, a scene that quickly turned confrontational when they both wanted the same beer. A "female cat fight" ensued. Aimed at young males, the spot had strong sexual overtones mixed with humour. The strategy, although entertaining to the target male audience, failed to get guys to buy beer. In fact, sales actually went down after this very expensive campaign. Ouch.

Although great creative that drives sales is a brilliant combination, good creative isn't the only factor in effective advertising. An example is Wal-Mart. Hardly the hallmark of creative brilliance in their print and TV campaigns, their advertising is nevertheless very effective. London Drugs is another example. Product and price advertising through regular flyer distribution in community newspapers is a proven vehicle to drive sales. Is the creative for Walmart and London Drugs memorable? Not particularly, but the ads drive sales and that's what makes them good.

Beyond a well-understood target audience and an appealing message, the media choices made can make or break a campaign. Internet advertising, a media vehicle much hyped before the dot. com bust, has come of age. Now, rather than transferring traditional methods to this medium, the advertising community is applying new and creative strategies which would not be possible in other media vehicles.

The interactive use of the Internet to engage the individual consumer is one progressive example. Another revolutionary development is happening at the search engine Google. We now have the level of sophistication and technological capability to understand how it could change the context of media buying. It's called "Internet-based contextual advertising." Contextual advertising serves up ads online to individual web page viewers. But here's where the spin changes. The ads viewed are based on the content the viewer is reading. The technology uses keywords associated with the advertisers' products or services. This media is transparent, accountable, and measurable. Google currently has over 150,000 active advertisers.

Truly effective advertising relies on the success of a well-defined and understood target group, clear objectives, a resonating message, and effective media choices.

Branding and Your Competitive Advantage

■ ■ ■

Branding is at the very root of marketing. On the outside, your brand is the combination of name, words, symbols, and design that identifies you and distinguishes you from competitors. You reinforce your brand positioning through choices in location, services, pricing, selection, and quality. But it is what is on the inside of your brand that defines the emotional connection. After considering the commonalities of truly great brands and considering how they align their brand promise with what they deliver, I think great branding comes down to one thing - emotion. Think of brands people are passionate about: Apple, Westjet, Lululemon, Vancity, Mountain Equipment Co-op. There is passion because there is an emotional connection. If you are able to establish an emotional connection with your customer, through shared values and experiences, you are well on your way to having a great brand.

Identifying and securing your competitive advantage in the marketplace is the key to business success. This process is tied very closely to creating the brand identity. Get these two elements right and you'll be unstoppable!

How to Give Your Brand an Enduring Competitive Advantage

■ ■ ■

Business in Vancouver newspaper, October 2, 2007

When most businesses launch, they claim a niche based on some sort of competitive advantage. As they become more successful competition usually moves in. It is at this point that many businesses fail. Why? Success depends on two factors: market share and distinct competencies. While still building market share, many failing businesses discover that their distinct competency is easily copied, or that they haven't yet established an emotional connection with their customers. Worse yet, if they haven't positioned themselves to compete on price, they are forced into this position, which results in shrinking margins. Brands need to go quickly beyond the functional benefits of what they offer to the emotional benefits of shared values and passions. This emotional connection will ensure your brand identity and positioning are secure in a competitive environment.

But first let's talk about market share. It's a simple concept. You want as much as possible. And you want to gain it in your category early. It's easier to have it and keep it than to steal it from competitors. Your distinct competency can be in one or several of these areas:

> Research and development expertise
> Manufacturing processes

> Marketing skills
> Consumer segment knowledge
> Secure sourcing
> Distribution systems
> Unique reputation
> Brand capital

Distinct competencies can change, of course. No business is static. Suppliers change; distribution systems can be affected by new ownership or competitors. Evolving technology and legislation can change manufacturing processes. Consumer segments mature, trends take hold, change happens. The key is to have a distinct competency that is not easily copied. If you are successful, you will get competition. Brands with the largest market share and strongest distinct competencies are in the best position to sustain competitive advantage. You also need to be vigilant in scanning information that could affect your industry. You always need to be one step ahead of change.

Where good brand become great brands and where businesses are best positioned to deal with competitors is when they have moved beyond functional benefits and have connected with customers on an emotional level. Brands move through a spectrum where customers first gain awareness, then develop a preference. Typically, this is based purely on the functional aspect of your offer. A person might need a coffee on the way to work. Your business is on their route, you sell good coffee, bingo! You have a new customer. You keep them initially because your coffee is good, it's hot, and it's convenient. Establishing an emotional benefit with that customer will allow your brand to move further along the spectrum to insistence and finally the golden grail, obsession. This is when your brand shares values and passions in common with your customer. In our coffee example that might mean connecting with social responsibility values through the use of free trade coffee only or being known as an employer who embraces diversity and cares about employees. It might mean giving back to the community or reducing your environmental impact. These are all potentially emotional hot buttons that can establish a bridge with customers. When staff know people by name, take the time to chat or give out free samples, suddenly they are more than just a coffee source, they are a morning ritual, just like meeting up with a friend. Making your business and brand more personable helps form an emotional bond.

"A brand has to feel like a friend," notes Howard Schultz, chairman and CEO of Starbucks. Friends share emotional connections. Wise words from the coffee world, but they can apply to all businesses.

The final key to unlocking a successful brand position is to take the brand identity, with strong distinct competencies, established market share, and an emotional connection with customers, and package it in a memorable way.

A Brand Is More Than an Identity; It's a Promise to Deliver a Positive Experience

■ ■ ■

Business in Vancouver newspaper, May 31, 2005

Good branding is important to successful marketing. But what really is good branding? Most of us recognize it when we see it or experience it, but few of us truly understand how to effectively create it. The dictionary defines a brand as a product or service bearing a widely known name, something distinguished by distinctive characteristics. Although accurate in some respects, this definition is devoid of emotional character, which is at the heart of good branding. Duane Knapp, president of Brand Strategy Inc., believes that good branding starts with asking the questions, "How are you going to be perceived as distinctive? And most importantly, what is your brand promise?"

Knapp notes, "Birks' brand promise is to surprise and delight," not just sell jewellery. The emphasis is on the customer experience while buying jewellery. More important than what or how you sell is the identification of how you will make your customer feel. "A brand has to feel like a friend," notes Starbucks CEO Howard Schultz. These are wise words. Superior and well-loved brands evoke an emotional response. People light up and get excited when they speak of experiencing them. Lululemon, Starbucks, and Birks come to mind. These brands have an attitude and a mindset that makes the experience memorable. Number one brands have three things in common:

1. They are possessed by how their customers feel. They know what their customers are thinking daily.

2. They own a distinctive position in the marketplace. They offer benefits that their competitors do not.

3. That distinctiveness, what it stands for, is focused on functional and emotional benefits. They don't just deliver goods or services; they evoke an emotional response.

Without a brand strategy, you become a commodity, forced by competitors to compete solely on the merits of price. So how do you create a brand strategy?

1. Conduct a brand assessment: Get feedback. Learn how satisfied your customers are. Better yet, learn how delighted they are. Being satisfied fulfills a functional response. Being delighted feeds an emotional response. Compare yourself to competitors. Ask, "How do our customers think about us? How do they think about us relative to our competitors? And how do they think about us versus who they think is the best?"

2. Identify the distinct advantages and value you deliver compared to your competitors.

3. Identify your brand promise. Your promise is the heart, soul, and spirit of the benefits you deliver. A promise is never about your product or services; it's about how you want to make people feel. The promise sets the tone.

And remember you must invest time to teach your employees how to deliver "your promise." Part of the reason why Starbucks has been so successful is because they spent ten times more on training than advertising during the first ten years of business. They realized that conveying their promise through their employees was essential to building their brand.

FedEx is in the shipping business. They distinguish their product with pickup and delivery at any time, from any place. They deliver superior value by guaranteeing, "It will absolutely, positively get there on time." But their brand promise has nothing to do with delivering packages. Their promise is immediate gratification. When you deal with FedEx, you are confident that they will take care of it. Lululemon is in the athletic apparel business, but their brand promise is to help you enjoy life and make the world a better place. "We believe that if we can produce products to keep people active and stress-free, the world will be a better place. We aspire towards elevating the world from ordinary to a place of greatness," says company founder Chip Wilson. Starbucks is in the coffee business, but their brand promise is to deliver what they call a third place, or an escape. While coffee may be the primary product attraction, they offer a meeting place, somewhere to be at home without being home.

Far too many businesses today compete as commodities, battling for customers on the merits of low prices. Good branding makes your offering so much more competitive and ultimately more valued.

Marketer of the Year: Vancity Offers a Case Study in Effective Marketing

■ ■ ■

Business in Vancouver newspaper, October 18, 2005

What makes good marketing great? What are the company traits that score favour in customers eyes? And just what does it take to be awarded "Marketer of the Year" by the B.C. chapter of the American Marketing Association (BCAMA)? To qualify, winners must have a British Columbia - based marketing team, as well as an exceptional marketing strategy executed with notable results. This year's Marketer of the Year award winner, Vancity, treated over five hundred attendees to a compelling display, which showed them why the credit union was deserving of the honour.

Good marketing starts with solid branding, and an acute awareness of "the brand promise." The brand promise identifies how a company will make their customers feel. Superior and well-loved brands evoke an emotional response. People light up and get excited when they speak of experiencing their favourite brands.

But when was the last time you got teary-eyed with emotion when you thought about your bank? Exactly. However, as Vancity likes to point out, they are neither a bank nor a traditional credit union. As they saw it, there was a huge emotional branding void to fill in the banking industry. And it made great business sense. But the challenge was to translate already positive sentiments into business results. Thus begins the Vancity story.

■ ■ ■

A year ago, Vancity embarked on the process of envisioning and storytelling. This may sound a little touchy-feely for a bank, but it was a creative way for two thousand Vancity staff and board members to explore what the organization really stood for and what services it was exceptional at. The vision and storytelling were essentially their brand audit and assessment. They learned how satisfied their employees and customers were. They compared themselves with competitors. Their story helped explain who they were, what made them special, and what distinguished them from competitors. They then identified the distinct advantages and value they delivered compared with their competitors.

The results of Vancit's staff and board members' analysis defined the direction of their brand and became their inspiration for developing and executing their marketing strategy. The specific advantages and value they offered helped them identify their brand promise. They knew they had discovered the heart, soul, and spirit of the benefits they were delivering. Their newly defined brand promise was all about how they would make customers feel. It would set the tone. Vancity knew they had emotional equity with their customers. The challenge was to turn the high percentage with positive perceptions into increased business success. Their objective was to increase membership from one person in eight to one person in six, and to forge deeper and more diverse relationships with existing members.

They did this through several initiatives. They redesigned their logo to make it more approachable. They designed their branches to reflect more aspects of members' lives with the addition of things like bike racks and hitching posts for dogs. They sponsored the U-Pass, the University of British Columbia's discounted student transit ticket. They initiated banking firsts that would appeal to their potential customer base - these included clean-air auto loans, innovations and bright ideas for business loans, the self-employed mortgage, and free online bill payments. They embarked on a multimedia advertising campaign used in print, radio, TV, online, and billboards. All of these inventive enterprises challenged perceptions in the banking industry and invited customers to "expect better" at Vancity.

"Segments traditionally underserved in the banking industry - such as youth and the gay and lesbian markets - were targeted with great success," notes Kari Grist, VP of marketing for Vancity. Both these markets were of long-term growth value. The new, shared success program gave back a percentage of profits to members, which in turn increased the amount of business they did with the credit union.

Vancity conducted its brand audit from late 2003 to early 2004 and launched its marketing campaign in February 2005. Since then, it has racked up the following results, which Grist feels were largely influenced by the company's original marketing initiatives:

> A 1% jump in market share from 2003 to 2004.

> The under-25-year-old customer made up 20% of the member base in 2005, which was up from 17% in 2003.

> The 21% gay community market share increased by 15% between 2003 and 2005.

> Surveyed 86% member satisfaction in 2004.

> The number of members who left the bank (the churn rate) was 2.5 times less than Vancity's competitors. This number

decreased during the time of the campaign.

> *Maclean's* magazine named Vancity the best Canadian employer to work for in their October 2004 annual Top 100 Employers ranking.

> 30% of profits ($17.9 million) were returned to members and the community in 2005, based on the performance of 2004.

∎ ∎ ∎

Vancity is a strong brand. And with their latest marketing strategy, they have successfully demonstrated how to convert emotional equity into increased business success. Their customers' interests, feelings, and reactions are nearly an obsession with Vancity. They know what their customers are thinking daily. They own a distinctive position in the marketplace. They offer benefits that their competitors do not. That distinctiveness - what they stand for - is focused on functional and emotional benefits. They don't just deliver goods or services - they evoke an emotional response. In short, they do well what a good brand should do.

And now a confession: I believe that only Vancity could get away with having a drag queen MC and buff young men dashing gallantly throughout the crowd handing out Ginch Gonch Vancity Underwear to current bank members at a Marketer of the Year awards ceremony. Vancity is not an ordinary bank. And they're happy to belong to that extraordinary group of companies that treat their customers as few other companies do.

Former High-Flying Air Canada Hits New Marketing Low

■ ■ ■

Business in Vancouver newspaper, June 28, 2005

I've never met the CEO of Air Canada. But if I do, I know what I would tell him. Air Canada's marketing misses the mark. To be more direct, they just don't seem to get it. There is something to be learned, albeit in a backhanded way, from the Air Canada example. Their latest lame attempt at marketing to lure me as a customer is so bad I just had to write about it.

I can imagine the banter in the Air Canada boardroom discussing ideas for the latest campaign: "Everyone needs food. We all buy groceries. So let's sell airfares like groceries and everyone will want to buy from us." The headline "Attention Shoppers" harkens back to the old K-Mart days when a tacky voice-over would inform you that there was a special on toilet paper in aisle nine. The print ad, appearing in the *Vancouver Sun* and other Canadian dailies, goes on to inform us that we buy options on cars and software, so why not airfares? The poor guy pictured in the ad remarks, "Options? I love options." No, he doesn't! Air Canada just thinks he loves options. The ad proceeds to outline in painful and complicated detail all the options: Tango, Tango Plus, Latitude, Latitude Plus, and Executive Class. It outlines how they will nickel and dime you for Aeroplan miles, or not, and Status miles, whatever those are, as well as priority treatment, or not, of you as a customer. When I first heard the radio spot for this campaign, I honestly thought it was a joke. I thought it was actors doing a spoof on Air Canada. I waited for the punchline and it never came. It would all be laughable if it wasn't so painfully obvious what was wrong.

1. All people want to be treated well. They want to be more than satisfied. They want to be delighted. That's what good brands do. Customers don't want to be given a choice of being treated as first or second class, and worse, they don't want to have to pay extra for the privilege of being treated well.

2. Nobody but a bunch of navel-gazing executives cares about the options and details advertised. It's similar to the cell phone companies fighting tooth and claw over the number of minutes and when and where customers can use them. We simply don't care. Make a simple offer. Meet our needs, not the company's needs. Exceed our expectations. And convey it all in an easy-to-understand manner.

3. And just what is Air Canada's brand promise? I have no idea. As a potential customer, that's a huge problem. Are they a premium brand or are they a discount commodity? This latest campaign makes them look like both. Absolutely no brand loyalty, and I would argue limited sales, could result from this campaign. Their promise, whatever it is, should be to put the emphasis on the customer experience. More important than what they sell is the identification of how they will make their customers feel. A brand should feel like a friend. Right now Air Canada feels like a distant acquaintance.

In marked contrast, and coincidently on the back of the same ad page in the *Vancouver Sun*, was a smaller and more effective ad for Westjet. The headline read, "Go ahead, pick any seat you want, except the pilot's." The ad is funny, irreverent, and offers a simple message about web check-in. The ad reinforces cheap air-fares, but not cheap treatment. The positioning statement below their logo says it all. "Westjet. It's nicer up here." Their brand promise is clear. We know what they stand for. The experience promises to be fun. If you have ever flown with them, you know they have employee buy-in. Everyone feels like an important customer at Westjet, because they are - even though they paid rock-bottom prices for their fare. And that's the point. Too bad Air Canada just doesn't seem to get it. The announcement at Air Canada should go like this: "Attention shoppers, you can buy an authentic first-class seat in aisle nine where we promise to gouge your pocketbook and treat you well, but you may want to consider the discounted seat, also in aisle nine, to the same destination where we promise to treat you poorly. Oh, and remember, if you want a smile and respect, we'll be glad to charge you extra." This campaign is a new marketing low for a company flying high in our skies.

A note to readers: Although Air Canada has long ago ended this particular campaign, they still promote optional services to their business travellers in exchange for scaled ticket prices. The company still flounders to position itself with the leisure travel customer. The latest move to charge extra for baggage in an attempt to recover costs from rising fuel prices represents yet another public relations blunder. And in a recent call to question why I hadn't received an e-ticket confirmation by email, a recorded message politely informed me that a $20 service charge might be applied to my account for my inquiry. Calin Rovinescu became CEO of Air Canada on April 1, 2009.

Brand Building Lululemon Style

■ ■ ■

Business in Vancouver newspaper, February 15, 2005

Brand building is key to a successful marketing strategy. Yet few companies truly understand just how to do it well. Lululemon Athletica is an exception. They understand that good branding goes beyond a great logo and advertising.

A quick survey of a recent issue of the *Georgia Straight*, Vancouver's entertainment weekly, reveals no less than twenty-four ads for yoga and related products or services. There are over thirty private yoga studios in Vancouver. And you'll see almost as many yoga mats as lattés in hand on the streets of Kitsilano. Clearly there is a serious yoga trend afoot in Vancouver. But you knew most of this. Yoga is hot, and nobody knows that better than Chip Wilson, CEO of Lululemon Athletica. His company is a brand-building success story.

Building a brand starts with a precise definition of the target customer group, its needs and expectations. Although the company makes clothing for both sexes, 70% of the product mix is catered to women. The typical Lululemon customer is female, age twenty-five to thirty-five, educated, professional, has a relatively high disposable income (their stuff isn't cheap), is active, socially conscious, environmentally aware, and open to spirituality.

Lululemon as a brand demonstrates a fundamental understanding of women. They get direct feedback from women on product design through their research and design program, which sponsors women athletes and instructors. They have catered their stores to the needs of female customers and employees. Fitting rooms are extra large to accommodate strollers, and most stores have a customer washroom facility and play toys for young kids. They understand that shopping with children is a reality for many of their customers. Women staff most stores, and the company has initiated a workplace job sharing program.

The next step in building a great brand is to decide what benefits are offered that will give the brand a distinctive position in the marketplace. Lululemon's goal was to provide comfortable clothing for yoga. When they started, much of what was available was for men and the materials were lacking in stretch and comfort. Lululemon products are now made from a unique stretch fabric developed by the company founder. The product design and fabric were unique to the market, and this remains the company's primary benefit over competitors.

Lululemon supports their product benefits with a clear understanding of their target market in all things they do. This is demonstrated through their understanding of how to market to women.

1. Women's purchase decisions are informed and deliberate. All employees are well trained and many are women. They are educators. They participate in yoga classes in their community. They live the lifestyle of their customers. Employees don't seem to push product as much as share with customers something they love.

2. Women talk. You want them to talk about your product in a positive light. Lululemon's target twenty-five to thirty-five female consumers are trendsetters and decision-makers. They notice clothing. If they like the product, they spread the word. Lululemon understands this and they know how to generate talk. Their website and newsletter are great examples. The newsletter features uplifting articles about healthy living and empowerment. As a position piece it is an extension of their brand without actually pushing product. Customers perceive that the company's values are aligned with their own. The product is based on a quality look and feel. This is not lost on their customer base. They're talking.

3. When women shop, they see everything. Store design, lighting, and accessibility are important. In Lululemon's case stores are stylish and easy to navigate. Service is attentive and knowledgeable. If the brand image and message don't match the experience, women will notice. The company understands that everything about the in-store experience is a further extension of their brand.

4. Understand that women crave an escape. A sheet included with every purchase reads like a manifesto for good living. Among its suggestions: "Dance, sing, floss and travel. Friends are more important than money. Compliments from the heart elevate the spirit." And an article in their newsletter leads with "Isn't it time to leave the circus?" Lululemon gets it. Many women crave an escape and they've delivered it. This is brand extension brilliance.

5. Save her time and keep it simple. Stores are designed to make purchasing informed and easy. Different cuts and styles are displayed and racked logically. Staff know their products and make suggestions. They're not pushy. They make the shopping experience simple and save customers time.

Lululemon has effectively targeted their market and positioned well the distinct benefits they offer. Building a brand is about promising to deliver a consistent set of qualities, standards, values, and experiences. Lululemon has done just that.

A note to readers: In December 2005 company founder Chip Wilson sold 48% of Lululemon to Advent International for $108 million. He remains as chairperson and is actively involved in day-to-day operations. Currently they have forty stores in Canada, thirty-eight in the US, seven in Australia. They plan to open sixty additional stores in Canada and the US in the next two years.

Brand Building 101

• • •

Business in Vancouver newspaper, April 6, 2004

Brand building and positioning are important parts of your marketing strategy. Your brand is the combination of name, words, symbols, and design that identifies your product or service and distinguishes it from competitors. Every product, service, location you offer, policy you create, price you set, and action you take honours and builds your brand, or potentially damages it.

Ever hear of *Nuvo* magazine? Few in the magazine or advertising business had six years ago. Yet in an industry littered with unsuccessful startups and overlapping lifestyle magazines, *Nuvo* has successfully branded and positioned themselves as a high-quality general interest quarterly national magazine. How did they do it?

Building a brand starts with a precise definition of the target customer group and their needs and expectations. *Nuvo* targets affluent, well-travelled, highly educated Canadians. Pasquale Cusano, magazine publisher and founder of Montecristo Jewellers, felt there was a need in the market for a glossy high-end national luxury magazine that would meet the expectations of this discerning group. The name *Nuvo*, derived from "Nuovo," means "new" in Italian. Chosen for its simplicity, it evokes mystery, a European flavour, and is a symbol of something refreshing, new, and different. Positioned as "Inspired by quality," the magazine features editorial content on culture, style, and celebrity.

A business must decide which of the benefits it can offer that will give the brand a distinctive position in the marketplace. The simple goal, to focus on quality, has guided every business decision and helped position the *Nuvo* brand.

The product itself exudes quality. Printed oversize on 90lb gloss stock from Germany and perfect bound, the average 144-page magazine lands like a book on the coffee table. This itself sets it apart from other lifestyle magazines. The decision to limit advertising to full page, full colour only and have a 60% editorial and 40% advertising mix makes it distinctive in an industry which typically loads advertising much heavier and chops it up with smaller ads. All editorial is original to *Nuvo,* and covers feature striking artwork by world recognized illustrators and photographers. Distribution, at 50,000 across Canada, is highly targeted through direct subscription, delivery to affluent Canadian households, and through hotels and airline lounges. Ad placement at $13,000 isn't cheap, but the company has successfully leveraged premium brand advertisers such as Chanel, Audi, Cartier, and Jaguar, as an extension of their own brand. Nuvo recently won the Benny Award for the best printed magazine in North America. Clearly the single focus on quality has given their brand a distinctive position.

All marketing, advertising, and positioning efforts must fashion an image around the brand that is consistent with the benefits and that will bring excitement and satisfaction to the target group. Alessandra Bordon, director of sales and marketing at *Nuvo*, says simply, "We are in our readers' world. One way we do this is by distributing through high-end hotels and airport lounges. We know from research that our readers spend on average 14 nights per year at hotels. They travel extensively." During their early years, *Nuvo* had an agreement with the *Globe and Mail* newspaper to deliver the magazine to select high-income subscribers. Today, a limited number are delivered to *Globe* subscribers but the main source is subscriber based and from preferred client lists of advertisers. They believe this last source builds brand loyalty and a strong association with advertisers and their target markets. *Nuvo* also creates exclusive events, such as a celebrity wine tasting at the Vancouver International Wine Festival, and niche events at the Montreal International Auto Show and the Toronto Film Festival to position their brand.

For *Nuvo*, building their brand has meant going beyond positioning their product with readers. Although advertising decisions are sometimes made at the business level, in many cases, advertising agencies make the advertising budget decisions for national campaigns. In a world where PMB (Print Measurement Bureau) reports and ROI (return on investment) rule, *Nuvo* has had a tough battle to establish market share. Meeting the needs and expectations of this customer group may prove their toughest branding challenge. Canadian Circulation Audit Board (CCAB) distribution audit and marketing research conducted by Millward Brown Goldfarb in 2003 has helped lend credibility. And by sponsoring industry events like BC American Marketing Association presentations, they are putting their product in the hands of decision-makers. But a national magazine launched in Vancouver by a founder without a publishing background has been a hard sell to Toronto and New York. And when the cost to produce the high-quality glossy has exceeded the revenue it produced until recently, as Cusano admits, agencies and competing lifestyle magazines can be excused for questioning its long-term viability. Still, great brands are built on passion, patience, and perseverance, and the founders of *Nuvo* certainly have all three.

So what can you learn from all this? Identify you target group and the distinctive benefits you offer. This is what will define your brand image. Building a brand requires a promise to deliver a consistent set of qualities, standards, values, and experiences. Every business decision you make needs to endorse your brand position.

Successful Companies Define Core and Supporting Strategies

■ ■ ■

Business in Vancouver newspaper, May 6, 2003

At the centre of every successful business is a well thought-out and executed marketing strategy. Fundamentally this strategy allows you to achieve the maximum positive differentiation over your competition in meeting customer needs. Your marketing strategy is based on the interaction of your business, the customer, and the competition. There are really only three core marketing strategies that a company may use: operational excellence, product leadership, and customer intimacy. Let's examine each of these and look at some examples.

1. Operational excellence:
Typically these companies offer mid-market products at the best price with the least customer inconvenience. Under this strategy, the proposition to the customer is simple: low price or hassle-free service, or both. Future Shop is an example of a company pursuing a best price strategy. Founded in 1982, they are now the fastest growing national retailer of consumer electronic and computer products, with more than 100 stores across Canada. Their marketing strategy is structured on high sales volume, driven by heavy price point advertising and low margins. Customer service and product knowledge are of secondary importance.

2. Product leadership:

This concentrates on offering customers the best product. Typically product leaders continue to innovate year after year. The primary competition is not about price or customer service, it is about product performance. Mountain Equipment Co-op (MEC) is a member - owned and directed retail consumer co-operative. Established in 1971 by a group of Vancouver mountaineers, they now have 1.8 million members worldwide and seven stores in major Canadian cities. Peter ter Weeme, senior manager, communications and marketing, states, "Our priority is to ensure that MEC maintains its edge in innovative product offerings." The company has developed its own extensive MEC clothing and Serratus packs, bags, and tents line. Today, 60% of goods sold at MEC are designed in-house. MEC tests fabrics and designs extensively through their own labs and through member feedback. Although functional clothing, presented in a classic style, has been the earmark of MEC designs, there has been an increasing focus on fit and fashion in recent years, with 95% of clothing now being available in both men's and women's styles.

3. Customer intimacy:

This strategy focuses not on what the market wants, but on what specific customers want. Businesses pursuing this strategy cultivate relationships and specialize in satisfying unique needs. Banyen Books in Vancouver is an excellent example of this strategy. Since 1970 the store has carried an exhaustive selection of books and recordings on personal growth and spiritual awareness. More than just a bookstore, they position themselves as a resource for learning and a sanctuary for discovery. In addition to more than 27,000 books, CDs, tapes, and videos, the store sponsors weekly author discussion events. Notes Kolin Lymworth, company founder and owner, "We cultivate the relationships once they come; we don't engineer it by tracking them." They are a single location, destination retail model. Although the core strategy positions the company, it is in combination with the supporting strategy that the intricacies and true competitive advantage often play out. Decisions in the areas of price, promotion, and distribution form the supporting strategy and reflect the particular strength of the company, the specific demands of the marketplace, and the competitive thrust. Defining the supporting strategies helps to further differentiate the business and defines the areas where they pursue competitive advantage.

To understand the concept of core and supporting strategies, let's take another look at Mountain Equipment Co-op. Although its core strategy of product leadership is at the basis of its business model, its marketing strategy is infinitely more complex. They further define their core product leadership strategy through supporting price, promotion, and distribution strategies. MEC positions itself as delivering value-priced quality products. Because MEC manufactures its own brands and realizes economies of scale on materials, its margins and prices can be much lower than traditional retailers in that sector. Where others might spend 4 to 6% of sales on promotion, MEC spends much less, instead choosing to focus its efforts on 1:1 communication with members through two annual catalogues and its website. The company relies heavily on word-of-mouth advertising. As a co-operative, they sell goods only to members, but anyone can join for life by purchasing a $5 share. This model makes their distribution system unique. Sales topped $165 million in seven national stores last year, and an eigth location is opening in Montreal this year. With the addition of a fully commerce capable website in 2001, their distribution system truly expanded to members worldwide.

E-commerce sales last year were $7 million. Although their catalogue was originally intended for a rural audience, it has become a critical marketing tool. Customers frequently pre-shop or order by phone after visiting a store in urban areas. Used in concert with the website to gain product knowledge and order goods, the catalogue is a key part of their multi-channel distribution strategy.

A final differentiating supporting strategy is one of values. The company has strong social and environmental principles, which guide everything from building enviro-friendly stores to the use of 30% post-consumer waste paper for their catalogue. Clearly MEC has a unique supporting strategy. Successful companies clearly define their core and supporting marketing strategies. The key, of course, is to select one that fulfills a market need and is not being met by competitive providers. Too many companies don't clearly define their strategy or select one, which does not adequately differentiate them from competitors. Business is not static. Your must reassess your strategy in light of environmental and competitive changes. That is how businesses succeed.

A note to readers: MEC currently has 12 locations across Canada. Their sales were $239 million in 2007. Their strategy has remained consistent, enabling their rapid growth, although increasingly they are manufacturing much of their clothing offshore in Asia.

Identify and Hone Your Competitive Advantage

■ ■ ■

Business in Vancouver newspaper, November 26, 2002

What is your competitive advantage? What are your distinct competencies? If you don't know, you'd better find out, and fast!

Most businesses carve a niche for themselves based on some sort of competitive advantage. This may be based on a unique product or service only available through their company. It may be based on an exclusive or unique channel sourcing or distribution system. It might be based on cost leadership. Some advantages are more easily imitated or challenged than others. Truly successful companies cultivate a unique competitive advantage, which is unlikely to be easily imitated.

Two attributes determine the strength of a company's competitive position: market share and distinct competencies. The larger the market share, the stronger the competitive position. A large market share provides experience curve economies and suggests the company has earned brand loyalty. The uniqueness, strength, and number of a company's distinctive competencies are the second measure of competitive position. Distinct competencies refer to things such as a company's research and development expertise, its manufacturing processes, marketing skills, consumer segment knowledge, secured sourcing and distribution system, or unique reputation and brand capital.

In general, companies with the largest market share and the strongest distinct competencies are in the best position to build and sustain their competitive advantage.

Let's look at an example from the Canadian retail sector. Book Warehouse is a Vancouver owned and operated discount bookstore with six locations in the Lower Mainland. The company is a cost leader with a focused competitive strategy. Their primary distinct competency is the management of remainder books. They have concentrated their product offerings in the area offering the highest margins. Remainder books represent a fraction of total sales but contribute substantially to total profits. Their unique approach is based on secure channel sourcing contacts and astute buying abilities. It is a competitive strategy which is unlikely to be easily imitated.

Kidsbooks, with locations in Vancouver and North Vancouver, have secured a unique position as knowledgeable and comprehensive suppliers of the children's book niche market. This has ensured their success in the face of competitive threats from big-box booksellers such as Chapters and Indigo.

In 2001, Chapters/Indigo's combined market share was estimated at an overwhelmingly dominant 70%. Yet, since the fall of 1995, when Chapters entered the Vancouver marketplace, both Book Warehouse and Kidsbooks have managed to increase their market share. In these particular examples you can see how having strong distinct competencies can thwart off fiercely competitive threats. Duthies' distinct competency of comprehensive selection, source ordering, and knowledgeable staff was seriously challenged with the entrance of Chapters into the Vancouver marketplace. Their brief change to category cost-leadership failed them when their business model couldn't sustain decreased margins. The company now has a single west side location, down from ten when it was known as a Vancouver bookselling institution.

Successful businesses go to great lengths to protect their distinct competencies from challenge in order to guard their competitive advantage. Is your business based on a distinct competency? Have you developed strategies should it become challenged? These are questions worth asking and answering. The only thing certain in business is change.

An update to readers: After fiercely battling each other for market share, Chapters and Indigo merged. Although the entrance of these two major bigbox book retailers knocked out many small independents across Canada, both Book Warehouse and Kidsbooks have survived and thrived largely because of their unique distinct competencies.

Marketing Planning and Strategy

■ ■ ■

This section covers a lot of "how-to" questions in marketing. I've looked at successful company case studies, and zeroed in on some strategy fundamentals. Far from textbook in the approach, the examples help illustrate areas such as competitive advantage, core competencies, pricing strategies, marketing plans, and the basics of good advertising. In addition to articles looking at what you should do, there are some articles that address what you shouldn't do. Learning from others' mistakes costs you nothing!

Why You Need to Create a Personal Marketing Plan

■ ■ ■

Business in Vancouver newspaper, September 26, 2006

Despite persistent folks wearing flip-flops, summer is officially over. The kids, and even some of us, are back in school. There's a general feeling of newness and enthusiasm in the air that greets us in the fall. What better time to assess, reflect, and plan for change? Although many of us are familiar with the idea of creating a marketing plan and strategy for clients or products, the idea of a marketing plan for ourselves seems foreign. But when you think about it, shouldn't you have a plan to market and sell what you do best in the marketplace?

If you were selling a new product or service, you wouldn't focus exclusively on what it had done for others in the past; you would tell people what it could do for them in the future. You'd create value. You'd create desire. You'd make people want to have it. And if you were selling against a competitor, you'd seek out market intelligence and know how to best position your product or service in the marketplace. The same principles apply to your own personal marketing strategy.

Minto Roy, president and CEO of Premier Career Management Group, advocates a distinctive approach to career management. PCMG, far from the traditional career placement agency, offers a unique blend of personal coaching and personalized matching of companies with business problems to the resources their clients are able to apply. PCMG actively seeks out businesses with needs. "They may not say they're hiring, but almost everyone has problems they need solved." PCMG simply helps people position their talents to create future value for prospective employers. Then they coach them on how to sell their features and benefits. Roy says, "Our clients have better market preparation, and in a one-hour interview, they're better prepared to win the race." Although many of PCMG's clientele are new immigrants, the model they use can be applied by anyone at any stage of their career.

If you're looking for employment, instead of relying on a résumé of what you have done, research the companies you want to work for and present them with a plan to solve a problem. Same thing applies if you are underemployed or looking for advancement with your current company. Know how to position yourself in the marketplace. Create value. Know your competitive advantage and the distinct features that make you unique and desirable. Then position those features in your competitive environment. Here are the issues to address in your personal marketing plan.

1. Your environmental analysis: Look at competitive forces around you. Assess the economic, political, regulatory, technological, and sociological influences in your industry.

2. Your target market: Look at the demographics and psychographics of the people and companies you want to reach. Who are they? Where are they? What are their general personalities?

3. Your marketing objective: Do a personal SWAT analysis. Look at strengths, weakness, opportunities, and threats. Match your strengths and opportunities, and convert your weaknesses and threats.

4. Your personal marketing mix: Decide who you are as a product. If you were a brand, what would you stand for and how would you make people feel? Know what you can offer that nobody else can. Decide what it will cost for an employer to hire you. Know where you will be seeking opportunities and how you will promote yourself.

5. Implementation: Organize your approach, responsibilities, and timetable for completion of your goals.

6. Evaluation and control: Set your own performance standards and financial goals. Monitor your progress. Know when to ask for change or advancement and know when to move on.

Having a personal marketing plan means taking control and responsibility for your own success. We do it for products and services all the time. Make now the time to do it for yourself.

The Seven Habits of Successful Marketers

■ ■ ■

Business in Vancouver newspaper, January 10, 2006

While just recovering from the festivities of the holiday season, and ushering in the New Year, our focus at this time often turns to a fresh start. What better time to consider the elements of inspired marketing leadership? With a nod to Steven Covey and his "Seven Habits" of success, I'll offer up my "Seven Habits of Successful Marketers." In working with clients over the years, I have observed common traits and behaviours of successful marketers and business leaders. Besides an invigorating entrepreneurial spirit, an amazing intuitive grasp of how business works, and a driving desire for success, they possess leadership traits which form the basis of their marketing success. Work these into your plan and make it your best year yet!

1. They have a clear vision of their company values, what they want the company to become, and how they will get it there. They believe their company has a responsibility to set a personal best in their chosen industry. Leaders of these companies inspire a vision that will be shared by all employees. Without vision there are no values. Without goals and objectives, there is no course. Leading businesses and marketers define their values, goals, and objectives and then make it their voice in their industry. When Chip Wilson launched Lululemon, his vision was "to elevate the

world from mediocrity to a place of greatness." He did this by providing yoga wear to help people lead a healthy, balanced, fun-filled life. Lululemon not only set out to be the best in their industry, but they grew from a single Kitsilano store in 1998 to over forty stores in Canada, the US, Japan, and Australia by the end of 2005. Lululemon also clearly defined their values. Who else could suggest you dance, sing, floss, and travel in their manifesto?

2. The company speaks with one voice to the marketplace. All marketing materials are integrated and aligned to support the vision. There is internal and external consistency. The customer knows not only what produce or service is represented, but the promise of what the business or brand will deliver. What does a small blue Birks box mean to you? That box speaks volumes. It promises something of quality and value. Most of all, it promises to delight. Birks has a clear, consistent voice. Their promise is clear.

3. They are pioneers in their industry, willing to step out into the unknown and search for opportunities to innovate, grow, and improve. They are not afraid to take calculated risks. When they generate a win, the business benefits. But they also learn from their mistakes. In the mid-eighties, did you think a smoke-free donut shop would have a future? Seems obvious now, but it wasn't when Tim Hortons first launched the idea.

4. They have a commitment to do better. They are not satisfied with the status quo. Whether it is becoming more innovative, giving better service, developing a better product, growing the business into new markets of opportunity, increasing efficiencies, increasing profitability, improving their marketing efforts, or simply making their business a better place to work for staff, they are driven to continual improvement.

5. They access accurate and timely information about the internal and external forces affecting their businesses. Successful businesses and marketers seek information about how their business is doing (the internal part) and then evaluate it in the context of what competitors are doing, what is happening to their industry, and what opportunities or threats might come up due to trends (the external part). Knowledge is king. They appreciate that business is not a static thing. It changes and evolves. Think of the camera and film industry, book sales, telecommunications, or post-secondary education as examples. All of these industries have seen huge external forces affecting their businesses. Nobody is free of influence. Leaders understand that unless you embrace constant threat and opportunity, you will get left behind.

6. They hire good people and give them the tools to be successful. They foster collaboration and build trust. They understand the value of ongoing training. They give employees the tools to do their job exceptionally well. They know how to empower their people. And they understand intuitively that their largest asset is people - both the people who work there and the customers they serve.

7. They understand the importance of good communication. This includes communication both with customers and with staff. The most successful companies are the ones who remain accessible and accountable. They think of everything as communication: their advertising, customer service, staff training, team building, and management relations.

Companies flounder daily for failing to address even some of these points. Forming habits first takes knowledge, then commitment, and finally change and practice. Make this the year to become the true marketing success you know you can be.

Time Is Your Customers' Most Valued Currency

■ ■ ■

Business in Vancouver newspaper, April 5, 2005

A recent time use study at the University of Maryland found that for the first time ever, more people said they were pressed for time than for money. This is a wake-up call for marketers. The very task of consuming takes time. Browsing, comparing, and researching are time-intense activities. Even the act of viewing advertising and filtering marketing clutter takes time. Time-respectful marketing is now key. You must view every action with the currency of time in mind. Yes, think of time as a currency. Your customers do.

1. Time-respectful advertising:

Does your marketing reward customers for their attention? Beyond the premise of a great product or service in the future, your marketing has to be time worthy. Think back to advertising that was memorable and motivated you to buy. It likely had an entertainment component, perhaps some humour, and it resonated with you in a personal way. When your customer's time is at a premium, this reciprocity element becomes critical. Alvin Wasserman, president and creative director at Wasserman Partners Advertising, says of the advertising process: "We're always looking for emotional triggers. We keep that at the forefront.

A creative brief will have all the reasons to buy listed, but once you answer the emotional triggers, you've got something that works. You'll make the connection." The sentiments of busy women are accurately portrayed in Wasserman's current London Drugs radio spots where a woman says, "I am not a shopper. I'm an individual. I want to come in, get what I want and leave." Identifying with the truthfulness that not all women are born to shop and many are short on time is the emotional trigger in this spot. If your advertising is entertaining and resonates on an emotional level with your target audience, you will earn the precious time and attention of customers. When time is more valued than money, you can bet your customers will be frugal with it. Make your advertising time worthy.

2. Time-respectful products or services:
You need to take the time to experience your business as a customer does. Look at every interaction with a new set of eyes and be critical. How long do you get put on hold when you call in? How quickly do you get service when you want it? Are your hours convenient? How complex is your return process? Can a customer come in, find what they need, and exit quickly? Could you reduce the amount of time it takes a customer to install, learn, or understand your product or service? You should identify all potential time-wasting bottlenecks in your business and reduce or eliminate them. If waiting is unavoidable, make sure the time spent is entertaining or an enjoyable break in the day. Make them understand that you value their time.

Mr. Lube offers customers a coffee and paper while they wait for an oil change. Wait time becomes break time. Book Warehouse hands out savings coupons to customers for their next purchase if the line at the cash register becomes too long.

Goodwill buys time. Consumers short on time are also looking for convenience. Why else would stores like Walmart sell bread, milk, and quick-prepared dinner items at their checkout? At the Yaletown Urban Fare you can shop for specialty grocery items and then not bother to prepare them and instead enjoy a dinner at the city's only licensed supermarket bistro. This offering of groceries and restaurant is aimed directly at the time-starved urbanite.

Nandini Venkatsh, marketing director for Ikea Canada, notes, "We're all time starved. We don't have enough time. We want convenience and we want to do it all in one shopping experience." She believes the ability to meet this need is a cornerstone of Ikea's success. By offering ten thousand articles under one roof and the convenience of online shopping, Ikea can save their customers time by offering the opportunity to accomplish all their home décor and gift giving shopping needs at one store. What time-saving services or convenience items could you add to your offerings to make your business more appealing to the time starved?

Until someone finds a way to sell time in a bottle, you need to ensure that your advertising, products, and services are respectful of your customer's most precious currency - time.

SFU, GM Get Good Mileage Out of Business Project

■ ■ ■

Business in Vancouver newspaper, December 14, 2004

Take a group of university students, a car, and the knowledge and ingenuity to pull off a promotional stunt and what do you get? If you're thinking of UBC engineers hanging a Volkswagen off the Lions Gate Bridge, try again. Think business. Think *The Apprentice.* Think SFU. Recently students at Simon Fraser University in Burnaby, BC, got to tackle a real marketing challenge with a real budget, real customers, and a real client. The class of fourth-year business administration students worked in teams *"Apprentice* style" for a client every bit as demanding as Trump himself. The twist? Nobody got fired, and everyone increased their chance of being hired in the marketing field based on their experience. They were participants in the General Motors Marketing Internship Program facilitated by program administrator EdVenture Partners.

This is GM's second year participating in the Canadian program, having been involved for fifteen years in the US. EdVenture Partners, launched fifteen years ago in the US, is the bridge between academic institutions and corporate business. The goal of the program is to take the academic business model and apply it to the real world. "We've worked with four hundred colleges and universities in Canada and the US and have had thirty-five thousand students go through our program since we started," notes EdVenture CEO Tony Sgrow. To date, ten schools in Canada have participated. Simon Fraser is the first university in British Columbia to be involved.

The class was divided into teams to tackle strategy, research, advertising, public relations, finance, and project coordination. Together their work simulated that of an advertising agency for the client. The challenge was to take a budget of $3,200 and use it creatively to increase the awareness of the Chevrolet Aveo. The process they followed is a great template for approaching a promotional marketing event.

1. They did their research. They conducted qualitative and quantitative research through focus groups and self-completed questionnaires with a diverse representation of students on campus. Things such as awareness and perception of the Aveo brand, awareness and perception of competing brands, and a measure of attributes that influence purchase decisions were calculated before and after the event. Preliminary research indicated that the Aveo had a relatively low level of awareness and that Asian imports were favoured over the GM brand. Price and reliability were identified as key attributes of importance.

2. They developed a strategy for the event. The goal for the promotion was to increase the awareness and stimulate a positive perception of the Aveo on campus. To accomplish this, they set out to put "six hundred cheeks in seats" to get students to experience the spacious and stylish interior of the car. The theme for the campaign became *"More* than you think." They created a single-day event that featured live music, free food, and a contest. For each person who sat in the car, a package of Kraft Dinner was donated to the SFU and Greater Vancouver food banks.

3. They made an advertising plan. Pre-event advertising included campus banners, posters, in-class presentations, flyers, website exposure, an email campaign, and cheeky T-shirts worn by the class for the week prior featuring two cars strategically placed across the chest with the words "MORE than you think." On event day they had more banners, sandwich board people, flyers, Aveo display cars throughout campus, and projector screens with information, Aveo commercials, and a live slide show of the event. They made contest winner information and event photos available on a website. They calculated expected impressions to measure exposure.

4. They developed a public relations plan. Their budget was tight, so they made a strategic effort to cultivate publicity before, during, and after the event. They identified media outlets to approach and key contacts. Utilizing the strength of their association with SFU, they had the first set of press releases sent via the university's PR department.

5. They had a financial plan. At $3,200 the budget wasn't big and they accounted for every last penny. They sought sponsorships and donations to create value.

6. They had contingency plans. They addressed, controlled, and anticipated problems and put a plan in place for each scenario.

The results? On November 9, more than 684 students sat in the Chevrolet Aveo, and seven hundred items of Kraft Dinner were donated to the SFU and Greater Vancouver food banks. Class members working at Ipsos - Reid as part-time co-op students conducted the research analysis. Their post-event research indicated 40% of 17,000 students on campus were aware of the campaign. Most importantly, the awareness of the Aveo brand had doubled, and they were able to show a positive shift in perception of key attributes such as reliability.

On November 30 the students got to present their findings to the client, General Motors, and senior faculty. The project, based on curriculum-based peer marketing, at first glance appears to offer companies such as GM an exclusive and valuable low-cost method to access and persuade a valuable segment of their target market. It certainly challenges school administrators to strike the proper balance for the sponsoring business's involvement in curriculum development. In fact, EdVenture Partners CEO Tony Sgrow freely admits the environment for corporate participation on Canadian campuses is more rigid than in the US.

Program champion and faculty instructor for the Business 448 Advertising and Promotion class Cathy Ace notes the students have grown tremendously from their experience. "They've learned how to work as a team, handle tight budgets, manage their time, and meet deadlines. This project was the lab for the business student. It's so much better than a case study." In addition to getting real hands-on experience, students are positioned better for a competitive marketplace. "I've had a client hire directly from a presentation," notes EdVenture's Tony Sgrow. The program delivers experience and better job prospects for the students. The sponsoring client gains valuable marketing insight and exposure. The university involved is profiled as progressive and innovative. And now *you* can benefit from their approach for you next promotional marketing event. Everyone wins.

Successful Business People Have Common Traits and Behaviours

• • •

Business in Vancouver newspaper, June 1, 2004

I have the pleasure of meeting and working with new business people regularly. Many inspire me with their invigorating entrepreneurial spirit, their intuitive grasp of how business works and their driving desire for success. Working with these individuals to improve their marketing efforts is truly satisfying. I have observed common traits and behaviours of the successful ones, and without exception there are eight things they all do well. To a large extent these behaviours form the basis for their success. Let's check to see how your business measures up.

1. They have a clear vision of what they want to become and how they will get there. Without goals and objectives, you will simply drift rather than chart a course. In nautical terms a drifting business is prone to crashing or running aground. These people understand that their chart, compass, and course are like a vision, with objectives and a plan. They don't leave home without them.

2. They have a commitment to do better. They are not satisfied with the status quo. Whether it be giving better service, becoming more innovative, increasing efficiencies, increasing profitability, growing the business into new markets, improving their marketing efforts, or simply making their business a better place to

work for staff, they are driven to continual improvement.

3. They know their numbers. If they don't have a financial background they hire someone who can give them the information they need to make informed decisions about their business. They measure everything: gross sales, margins, expenses, profit, inventory, sales per square foot, and stock turns. They know their numbers for every location and every business unit. They have estimates for their competitors based on sound competitive intelligence. They monitor their numbers daily and track monthly and yearly trends. They are able to recognize when change has occurred and respond immediately.

4. They have good systems. Everything in business can be defined as a process, and every process needs a well-thought-out system to make it function efficiently and consistently. Their systems for payroll, ordering and processing, stock replenishing, communication, computer networks, and hiring and training staff have all been - well thoughtout and are constantly evaluated for improvement. They look at competitors' systems and they look at systems used in industries outside their own. They know that poor systems will hurt their business and they constantly look for ways to improve their own.

5. They get accurate and timely information about the internal and external forces affecting their businesses. Knowledge is king. Successful people seek information about how their business is doing (the internal part) and then evaluate it in the context of what competitors are doing, what is happening to their industry, and what opportunities or threats might come up due to trends (the external part). They appreciate that business is not a static thing; it changes and evolves. They understand that unless you embrace constant threat and opportunity, you will get left behind.

6. They understand the importance of good communication with staff and customers. The most successful are the ones who remain accessible and accountable. They think of everything as communication: their advertising, customer service, staff training, team building, and management relations.

7. They hire good people and give them the tools to be successful. They understand the value of ongoing training. They provide staff with the tools to do their jobs exceptionally well. They know how to empower their people. And they understand intuitively that their largest asset, their employees, leave the building to go home every night.

8. They have a clear definition of responsibilities. They know who will do what, by when, and with whom. This all ties back to their vision and their goals and objectives to get them there.

Simple points? Perhaps. Easily attainable? Hardly. Companies go out of business every day for the failing to address even some of these points. It takes many combined behaviours and skills to be truly successful.

Westjet Soars on Its Price-Leading Strategy

. . .

Business in Vancouver newspaper, September 23, 2003

All businesses strive to be powerful and profitable. To achieve this from a marketing perspective, you must own something your competitors do not. There are really only three things that can set you apart:

1. Delivering the lowest price and lowest cost structure.
2. Having an excellent product, location, or service.
3. Owning the relationship by delivering a superior experience.

Let's look at one of these - having the lowest price and cost structure - and see how this strategy can be used to achieve maximum differentiation over competitors in meeting customer needs.

The key to successfully implementing a price leadership strategy is to ensure you have an efficient and distinct cost structure. Since your profits are what are left over once your costs are subtracted, being the price leader without the lowest costs is a one-way ticket to bankruptcy. The uniqueness, strength, and number of distinct competencies that lower your cost structure are what make this strategy competitive. Since costs can be controlled at many levels, such as materials, manufacturing, maintenance, research, design, distribution, and human resources, there are many opportunities to structure a unique cost structure that is unlikely to be easily imitated. It has been demonstrated time and again that higher market share and experience lead to lower costs. If a business has a solid price leadership strategy that gains acceptance and momentum, it can be pretty hard to beat as it grows.

The airline industry is a tough, competitive environment, yet Westjet, a low-cost carrier, is one of the most successful airlines in Canadian history. Founded in 1996 by four Calgary entrepreneurs, it is now the second most profitable airline in North America, just after Southwest Airlines, a successful, US based low cost carrier. How has Westjet maintained a low cost model?

1. Lower staff costs: Pilot salaries are 75% of the industry average. Other staff salaries are 95% of the industry median. They offer generous stock options to compensate for this. In 2002 they paid out $15 million in profit sharing to employees. Westjet uses seventy-five employees to support each plane, whereas Air Canada uses 180. Westjet employees are also not unionized.

2. Lower maintenance and training costs: Westjet uses Boeing 737 airplanes exclusively. They stock parts and train staff based on one model of plane.

3. Lower food costs. They pioneered the snack and bag lunch option.

4. Lower ticketing costs and distribution overhead: Westjet was among the first to use direct consumer phone bookings and electronic ticketing. They were also leaders in online bookings.

5. More efficient flight schedule and service model: They use an A to B model rather than a web and spokes model, which is common with airlines such as Air Canada. Air Canada accumulates people in hub cities to get them to the spokes, which are smaller centres. There is a higher cost structure to support the one to two hours between flights for the hub and spokes model. Westjet, by efficiently providing a city-to-city service only, keeps non-flying time to a minimum and costs down. Clive Beddoe, president and

CEO, estimates that Westjet's costs are half of Air Canada's. Air Canada may lower their fares, paint the planes a different colour and brand them as Zip and Tango, but if the business model is not based on a low-cost structure, it cannot remain competitive as a low-cost carrier.

Every sector has a price leader. Price leaders can be challenged by new entrants who artificially lower their prices to gain market share. Since this practice is only sustainable over the long term by businesses with deep pockets, the truly successful businesses are those with a superior low-price strategy secured by a unique and controlled cost structure.

HMY Airways, an upstart Vancouver-based international airline, is positioned as a hybrid of the low-price/low-cost structure model. Launched in winter of 2002 as a vacation travel destination airline, their business model emphasizes operational efficiency, customer service orientation, and competitive pricing. While still in the early stages of introducing who they are, their initial success demonstrates that the competitive environment of business is not static.

Customer needs, regulations, competitors, and trends all affect change. To compete on price and remain competitive over the long term, you must control your internal cost structure and then monitor external influences.

A note to readers: When HMY Airways launched in 2002, the company appeared poised to offer competition in the low-price/low-cost structure model. With a subsequent name change to Harmony Airways, the company announced on March 27, 2007, that operations would be closed down in early April. They cited costs and the inability to scale the business model as reasons they could no longer compete. With gas price increases, we have seen Air Canada slash jobs and unprofitable routes, while recovering some increased costs with additional fees for luggage. Westjet will have to continue achieving greater efficiencies to maintain their price-leading strategy in this new environment. Arguably, their marketing focus recently has put less emphasis on price and more on service, as shown in the "Westjet employees are owners" campaign. The economic downturn will be tough on all businesses in the airline industry.

Privacy Legislation Raises Public Issues for Business

. . .

Business in Vancouver newspaper, December 13, 2003

Customer information is critical to a solid marketing strategy. Does your business maintain a database of names, addresses, telephone numbers, and demographic information or past buying behaviour of customers? Do you utilize direct mail or email as part of your marketing efforts? Do you plan to use the information you currently have about customers for any other purpose than it was collected initially? Have you ever allowed a third party, such as a supplier, mailing house, or research firm to utilize or maintain a copy of your customer information? If you answered yes to any of these questions, you need to familiarize yourself with the Personal Information Protection Act (PIPA) that came into effect January 1, 2004. For businesses that have not been involved in the evolution of the legislation, the changes in practices required may come as a surprise. Considering that a failure to comply can result in a fine up to $100,000, it's financially prudent to educate yourself. And since the very success of your business may hedge on the leveraging of data about your customers, this is important stuff! No business wants negative customer relations or compliance costs of responding to complaints.

Mary Carlson, director of BC's compliance Office of Information and Privacy Commission, has outlined the privacy compliance issues. As of January 1, 2004, PIPEDA the (Personal Information Protection and Electronic Documents Act) has applied to the non-federally regulated private sector. As of January 1, 2004, PIPA (the Personal Information Protection Act) is provincial legislation that applies to the collection, use, and disclosure of personal information by businesses, nonprofits, and private sector organizations in BC, except when PIPEDA applies. As a business owner, here's what you need to know:

1. You must identify the purpose for collecting information and collect only the information necessary for that purpose. You must inform the person you are collecting information from of the reasons why you want it, and you must obtain their consent if you decide to use the information for a purpose different than originally planned. Do you plan on conducting research from your database? If you haven't obtained consent in the past, you're going to have to get it before you can use your database for this purpose.

2. You must obtain consent before or at time of collection to use the information. This may be verbal, written, or by an opt-in or opt-out option. You should never obtain consent by deceptive or coercive means, and consent may not be a condition for supplying a product or service. For example, you would need consent on a contest entry form to use the information for anything other than to inform the winner of their status. You cannot withhold a product or service from someone unwilling to supply personal information.

3. You should limit the collection of information to what is reasonably appropriate to fulfill your identified purpose. Asking for a customer's age, income, or marital status to complete a warranty would be unreasonable.

4. You must limit the use of personal information, and disclose it only for the purpose which it was collected. You should retain

information only as long as necessary to fulfill the purpose it was collected for. Customers shouldn't be subjected to offers from another company who accessed the list.

5. Your data should be accurate and you should provide appropriate security to make sure it is not accessed by another party. Access to customer lists should be limited to individuals who understand the new legislation.

6. You must be able to provide access to personal information that you hold. Upon request you must be able to access an individual's personal information for them, explain how it is used, and list the organizations that have had access to their information.

7. You must provide individual recourse and remain open and accountable. Have a policy for how to deal with complaints, and use of information and access to it.

PIPA legislation does have a grandfather clause. Cappone D'Angelo, lawyer with McCarthy Tétrault, notes that although the legislation does apply to information collected before January 1, 2004, an organization may continue to use and disclose such information to fulfill the purpose for which it was originally collected. Drew McArthur, VP and privacy officer, Telus, notes if you purchase lists for your marketing efforts, you may want to get a signed document to warrant that the list has been "permission based" gathered to meet the new guidelines. You might want to check these two websites for further information: www.oipcbc.org (Officer of Information and Privacy Commissioner of BC) o www.mser.gov.bc.ca/foi_pop/Privacy/default.htm (Corporate Privacy and Information Access Branch). If you have specific questions or concerns, you should seek legal counsel.

All this needn't take the wind out of your direct marketing and sales efforts. In addition to making you compliant, it may cause you to increase your overall efficiency in the long run. If it's good for your customers, ultimately it's good for your business. You just need to learn to work within the 2004 guidelines.

Research

■ ■ ■

Great marketers realize that research is important. There has been a lot of change happening in the marketing research industry, most notably the influence of the Internet as a data collection tool for both qualitative and quantitative methods. Although it's important to be knowledgeable about research, it's more important to understand where, when, and how to use it. In the end, the numbers mean nothing unless they deliver an actionable result. It's also important to remember that informal research can be very valuable to marketers. Talking to customers, getting feedback from front-line employees, talking to those in your industry, and being involved and connected are very simple and practical ways to conduct research. An inquiring mind asks questions daily. More than anything, I think it's this type of attitude that is most important to those in marketing.

A Customer Who Complains Can Be a Business Owner's Best Friend

■ ■ ■

Business in Vancouver newspaper, September 21, 2004

Since gaining more customers is the ultimate goal of your marketing efforts, you must ensure the new ones you attract have a good experience. But even more important is to know you are retaining the customers you've got. Replacing lost customers costs five times more than hanging onto loyal ones, and loyal customers are typically more profitable than new ones. If you're losing previously loyal customers out the back door, you don't have a marketing problem, you have a customer relations problem. Although there are a number of reasons why customers leave, the most significant factor, one completely within your control, is customer relations. When the customer has a problem with your company, how do you handle it? Hopefully problems are infrequent, but when they do occur, how often do you successfully recover the relationship? Although marketing is essential to grow your business, don't spend a dime until you know you've got good customer relations and a high retention rate. Otherwise much of your marketing budget is likely to be wasted.

I read recently that 96% of people don't complain when they experience bad customer service, but they do tell on average ten other people. Many of these people simply leave quietly and take their business elsewhere. The sad part is, many businesses don't know why these customers have left. They are left scratching their heads, pondering increased marketing expenditures to lift lagging sales. Viewed in this light, the customer who complains is your friend. When problems arise, most customers are simply looking for three things: They want to be acknowledged and listened to. They want to be respected and feel valued, and they want some assurance that their concern is important and will be addressed. The customer might be totally unreasonable, but these three things still apply.

1. Customers want to be acknowledged and listened to. Most of us need to simply listen more and talk less. This mantra is critical for front-line employees when dealing with customers. You should welcome and encourage complaints. Most customers simply don't like to address problems, but they will tell others. If a customer takes the time to complain, consider it a gift. Shut up and listen. Your biggest challenge is to be proactive and solicit customer input when your service has failed them.

2. They want respect, and they need to feel valued. Treat customers fairly. All customers deserve respect, even the most unreasonable ones. They need to feel valued even if you feel hard-pressed to find any value in meeting their demands. Being respected and valued is a critical component to any relationship. And if you view yourself as being in a relationship with a customer, suddenly the way you communicate changes. Make that mind shift.

3. They want some assurance that their concern is important and will be addressed. It's all about valuing what the customer has to say. Not only is the concern important, but it likely has financial value, because as the statistics suggest, the person who talks shares their message with at least ten others. A single problem then multiplies exponentially. You should respond to concerns at the first point of contact. Nobody wants to be left hanging or passed from

person to person. Take ownership of the complaint and solve it. Mike Lipkin, president of Environics/Lipkin, notes that Starbucks has a unique way of teaching their employees to deal with customer concerns. It's called - what else - the "latte method."

L - listen to the customer's concern.

A - acknowledge that you have heard their concern.

T - thank them for bringing it to your attention.

T - tell them what you're going to do about the problem.

E - encourage them to come back.

Having good customer relations is critical to running a successful business. In fact, it can become your advertising. The most powerful and cost-effective advertising is the enthusiastic recommendation of delighted customers. In a materialistic world, when something powerful comes for free, it's worth pursuing. Achieving excellence in customer relations and problem recovery should be a priority. Then go blow the budget on marketing.

Customers Really Do Know Best, So Talk to Them!

■ ■ ■

Business in Vancouver newspaper, April 1, 2003

Businesses compete to serve customer needs. To establish a strategic edge over your competition it is important for your business to clearly define the market and customers you intend to serve. But what do these customers actually think about your business? And how are you seen in relation to your competition? Answers to these questions can produce strategic insight in your quest for competitive advantage and increased market share. Let's look at some methods you can use to measure customer feedback.

1. Mystery shopping. What kind of experience is your customer having at your business? Mystery shopping can reveal the answers. Traditionally it has been used to pinpoint gaps in sales staff service that would contribute to customer dissatisfaction and to gather competitive intelligence by shopping at competitors' outlets. Representatives from a market research company are hired to pose as customers and then critically evaluate their experience on a survey designed to measure criteria such as customer service, product pricing, displays, and layout of store. Elaine Hay of Campbell Edgar, a mystery shopping research company, notes that the clients who use this technique most successfully do it on an ongoing basis. It gives them snapshots over time to obtain averages, from which they build training programs to address their weaknesses. She notes that when their marks start increasing so to do their average sales per transaction.

2. Focus groups. Focus groups are a form of qualitative research that aim to obtain insights into consumer behaviour rather than to draw precise conclusions. Conducting focus groups that result in useful information and valuable perspectives requires both science and art. A skilled practitioner is a must. Typically eight to ten people whose opinions are relevant to the subject are assembled in a central location to be interviewed by a moderator over a time period of about two hours. Ellie Sykes of Market Explorers notes focus groups are an effective way to identify what is important to customers. Too often, she notes, quantitative customer satisfaction surveys are conducted on what a company thinks customers value. To properly conduct a customer satisfaction survey, a focus group should be conducted first.

3. Customer satisfaction surveys. The self-completed written or oral phone survey is one form of quantitative research, which attempts to rate the satisfaction level of customers. The purpose is to find out where gaps exist and where improvements could make the customer experience better. "Comb analysis" is a valuable technique to establish what gaps should be addressed. It involves surveying your customer base, ideally by an objective outside provider, to rate your business and whoever the customer perceives as your main competitor on a number of purchase criteria. By having the customer first rate the importance of each purchase criteria to them, you can establish where the gaps are between you and competitors. For example, suppose two criteria were product innovation and packaging. If results indicated the quality of the packaging was not highly valued, and yet your business scored high on this criterion, you could likely save money by lowering your standards to only slightly above your nearest competitor. If, on the other hand, results indicated product innovation was highly valued and your closest competitor scored higher than you, there is a gap that needs to be improved. This technique was used several years ago under the direction of my company, Charleson Communications, for the sales department of the *North Shore News*. "We were able to identify strategic areas to focus our sales efforts in 2003," notes Dee Dhaliwal, sales director.

4. Customer intercept survey. This technique can be applied at the retail level. Interviewers systematically intercept customers departing a store to ask them questions about their shopping experience. A survey can ascertain gaps in service offerings, determine the reasons for shopping where they do and also gain a customer profile. A professional researcher can help to properly word questions that will deliver useful results. Book Warehouse has conducted this type of research at all six of its locations. "It's a great way to get feedback on our stores, profile our customers, and measure advertising recall," notes Sharman King, CEO, Book Warehouse.

5. Internet e-panels and online surveys. This is a growth area. Why the move in this direction? More people are online, it's an effective way to reach difficult segments, and since 1991 phone survey response rates have declined by 5% a year. Steve Mossop, senior VP of Ipsos Reid, notes that online panels vary in size between two hundred and a thousand participants. Although the set-up cost for an online panel of $50,000 to $100,000 usually limits these to larger companies, results could be realized over a two-year time period. The distinct advantage is having a ready-made list of people to consult. This is particularly good if it's a hard-to-reach segment (example: elite runners in major Canadian cities). Online surveys offer quick turnaround, low fielding costs, and the opportunity for visuals or virtual reality. Attrition, replacement, and respondent bias are the limiting factors.

6. Employee feedback and talking to customers. Front-line employees and sales staff can provide valuable insights about your customers. Owners and management should meet with managers, staff, and customers often. David Goldman, of Boys' Co, a successful men's fashion retailer, says, "It's all about communication." He is at the stores every week talking to managers and customers. He keeps in touch with customers by keeping in touch with their culture. Making regular trips to New York, London, Paris, and Milan, he taps into trends through people-watching in stores, restaurants, and clubs; meeting with designers, listening to music; and reading magazines of his target customer. "It's our job to transpose the culture into the showroom," notes Goldman. Quite simply, this is only possible if you are in touch with your customers.

In business, knowledge is vital. Customer feedback can give you the necessary information to ensure your competitive advantage and strategic position in the marketplace. When did *you* last measure customer feedback?

Staying on Top of Business Trends Helps the Bottom Line

■ ■ ■

Business in Vancouver newspaper, February 11, 2003

As a Canadian, you can be excused for thinking environmental scanning might have something to do with tracking record-breaking temperatures or the accumulated rainfall in Vancouver. As a business person, you have a responsibility to make yourself aware of trends and changes that affect your industry and your company's survival. That in a snapshot is what environmental scanning is all about.

Long-range, solid strategic planning requires regular and rigorous analysis of influences on your business. To prosper in the midst of change, you must stay acutely aware of what could affect your industry and your company.

Scanning can take place at several levels. Macro-scanning is done for the interests of the entire company. Micro-scanning is done at the product or market level. Scanning must be sensitive to technological, political, economic, social, and regulatory changes. By forecasting potential changes, you can analyze strategic shifts in the environment and look at alternatives in order to make critical choices that will affect the long-term success of your product or business. What are the benefits of scanning?

1. It can help you to capitalize on opportunities rather than lose these to competitors. Chrysler was the first car manufacturer to officially introduce the minivan, having recognized that growing

families were putting increasing demands on the family sedan. The minivan was aimed at the baby boomer market trying to escape the station wagon image they had grown up with. Chrysler launched the minivan in 1983 and the rest is history. As first movers they sold 209,895 models in North America in 1984 and did not experience heavy competition until several years later as GM and Ford played catch-up.

2. Scanning provides an early signal of impending problems that can be diffused if recognized in advance. A recent Ipsos - Reid study revealed that 71% of Canadians have Internet access. Next to using it for email (91%), the most common use was researching a trip (59%). While a smaller segment is actually purchasing travel on-line, market forces will ensure this trend continues to grow. Air Canada now only accepts bookings made online or through a travel agent. Since the airline no longer pays commissions to travel agents on bookings, the agents collect a fee for the service from the consumer. Using an agent to book Air Canada flights now increases the costs of travel, while tickets booked online receive an additional small discount. The trend is toward a direct company to consumer delivery system. This signals a dramatic change in the business model for travel agents. Uniglobe notes that there has been a shift toward leisure travel and away from corporate travel because of the no commission system. Travel agents are being forced to restructure their business model and move toward niche markets such as adventure travel and cruising.

3. Scanning sensitizes your business to the changing needs and wishes of your customers. This point is critical in an increasingly competitive environment. Although stores such as Capers have made organic and natural products the focus of their business, traditional grocery stores are now responding to consumer demand. Local grocery store SuperValu has built organic food and

produce sections in their stores. Home delivery companies were increasingly capturing this market niche. The organic market is growing at an estimated 15% a year. Consumers demanded an organic alternative. The stores delivered.

4. Scanning signals to the public that your business is sensitive to its environment and community. *Shared Vision* is a monthly magazine that focuses on healthy living through social, physical, intellectual, and spiritual growth. The strong social values of its readership and the recognition that authenticity means your actions should be consistent with what you believe in caused the magazine to recently change to begin printing on 100% recycled, 100% chlorine-free paper. Scanning sensitized them to their environment (the publishing industry) and the community (their readership).

Environmental scanning will cause you to think and act strategically and that's how businesses succeed. Now that you understand why environmental scanning is critical, watch for my next column on how to implement it in your business.

A note to readers: Whole Foods has since entered the grocery store category, and IGA repositioned their brand as IGA Marketplace. Both of these competitors, through their store design and product offering, demonstrate how the demand for organic foods has gone mainstream. *Shared Vision* magazine has since changed ownership and was later rebranded as *Today's Vancouver Woman.* They suspended publication in spring 2009, a victim of depressed advertising revenue in the economic downturn. It's perhaps ironic that companies from the automotive industry, used as an example in the original writing of this article in 2003, are now facing a dramatic fight to survive. Even more ironic is the fact that in addition to financial pressures brought on by an economic downturn, it appears the failure to recognize future demand for environmentally friendly vehicles may well write the final chapter for some car companies. Could environmental scanning have saved them from this mess? Likely not entirely, however, the companies that spotted this trend early such as Toyota and Honda, will no doubt emerge in better shape once the economy recovers.

Lower Mainland Companies Use Environmental Scanning to Keep a Step Ahead

■ ■ ■

Business in Vancouver newspaper, March 11, 2003

A note to readers: Since this original article was written, many changes have taken place in the industries noted.

The shift to DVD rental format is complete. Amazon expanded beyond just books and there are many more online retail book competitors. Electronic book readers like Kindle are making electronic books user friendly. Sound Plus caught the initial wave of high-end flat-screen TVs, but price competitors such as Best Buy and Future Shop quickly turned the product into a commodity. Sound Plus repositioned their business in 2008 as a custom sales and installation provider for high-end homes. They closed their large retail showroom to focus exclusively on this niche. Following a change in management, the company was acquired in January 2009 by La Scala Home Cinema + Integrated Media. Most printing these days uses digital technology rather than film. Creo, a global developer of digital imaging, was acquired by Eastman Kodak Company in 2005. And we've seen growth in real estate properties targeting the over-fifty consumer. Viewed in hindsight, many of the trends identified in 2003 seem obvious now. This further illustrates the importance of monitoring and responding to change.

Environmental scanning causes you to be aware of trends and changes that affect your industry and your company's survival. In my last column I discussed why scanning is critical. Now let's take a look at how to implement it in your business.

1. Keep a tab on broad trends. Are there technological advancements that could change the compatibility of your product? Are their impending regulatory changes that could place restrictions on you? How might economic changes or shifts in currency values affect you? How do demographic trends effect you? For example, in technology you might look at shifts in market share, sales trends, and growth of emerging technologies. The shift from VHS to DVD and the shift from film-based to digital-based cameras are two technology trends that are dramatically shifting the business models of companies in those industries. Rogers Video notes that currently 40% of new release rentals are DVD based and 60% are VHS. In 2001, 15 to 20% were DVD. They expect 60% to be DVD in 2003. While library movies are still dominated by the VHS format (65 to 75%) by 2005 80% of movies rented are expected to be on DVD. Currently, with 93% of Canadian households owning a VCR and 30% owning a DVD player, the company has determined that the trend is broad and relevant and has therefore altered their product delivery format in response to changing consumer demand.

2. Determine the relevance of the trend. Not all trends will be relevant to your company. However, be cautious about only looking at trends in your industry. Often shifts and competitive threats emerge from previously non-competitive industries. The retail book industry has experienced serious competition from Amazon.com and more recently Amazon.ca. These companies do not have a physical bookstore, and they utilize a distribution system that was not available to consumers ten years ago.

3. Study the impact of the trend on your product or market. A trend could pose either a threat or an opportunity. Determining the impact of the change will help you mitigate threats and maximize opportunities. Remember that scanning involves not only looking for potential threats to your business, but also recognizing opportunities and maximizing them before your competitors do. Sound Plus, a leading home theatre and audio retailer, has witnessed a trend toward flat-screen TVs, away from the traditional CRT (cathode ray tube) technology. They note that Hitachi, one of the largest TV picture tube manufacturers in the world, will have ceased manufacturing large picture tubes within three years. 90% of TV sales at Sound Plus are for flat-screen technology. They recognized the growth in home theatre and flat-screen TV was going to shift their business model from one previously dominated by audio products. In 2000 they doubled their floor space with the addition of a second-floor 5,000 square foot design centre to feature both home theatre and audio product to maximize on this trend.

4. Forecast the direction of the trend in the future. Time to get out your crystal ball. Prepare possible scenarios and their potential impact on your business. In the early 1990s, Vancouver had eight large prepress film houses. Of these companies only Total Graphics and Supreme exist today and their business model has changed. Why? The design and film output environment changed drastically with emerging technologies, but for many of these companies their business model did not. Creo, a Vancouver-based company founded in 1983, is a worldwide leader in computer to plate printing, a process that completely eliminates the need for film to create printing plates. Emerging technologies can put some long-standing companies out of business or create new leaders. Environmental scanning can help put you on the right side of the impending change.

5. Analyze the momentum of the product or market in the face of the trend. If you took no action, what would be the impact? Should you become a first mover? Do you need to alter your product? Do you need to strategically assess your business model and make major changes?

6. Study the new opportunities that the trend appears to provide. Are there new business opportunities? British Columbia has the second-largest seniors population in Canada, with 496,000 over the age of sixty-five. That is expected to grow to over 841,000 by 2016 according to Statistics Canada. In response to this trend, for example, Concert Properties has capitalized on the aging baby boomer demographic through the construction of the O'Keefe in Vancouver's west side. The development has 183 suites to own or rent targeted at active seniors. It offers lifestyle choices tailored to the individual needs and preferences of its residents. This is a company capitalizing on a demographic trend. Author Michael Schell has co-authored a book called *I Don't Do Dishes* that demonstrates the need for more seniors housing, complete with testimonials.

7. Relate the outcome of the environmental trend to the corporate or marketing strategy. This may cause you to make changes in your current products or markets or embrace opportunities.

Yes, you're saying, that's all fine for large corporations, but I don't have the time to do this in my small business. No problem. You likely do much of it informally already by reading industry publications, keeping up on current affairs, and networking. However, I challenge you to set aside time on an ongoing basis to formalize the process. You'll be surprised at how, in a very short period of time, you have become more attuned to your business, your competition, and your environment. Environmental scanning will cause you to think and act strategically, and that's how businesses succeed.

Competitive Intelligence Builds Base for Business-Winning Strategy

■ ■ ■

Business in Vancouver newspaper, January 14, 2003

Before you go off and hire James Bond to snoop around your competitors, let me explain. Competitive intelligence is the systematic and ethical collection and analysis of information to turn it into knowledge and strategy. You don't need to hire a detective to get it. You do, however, need to make a concerted and organized effort to acquire information and need to do further analysis to make it actionable. In order to decide your company's competitive moves, you must be aware of the perspectives of your competitors.

CI goes beyond industry statistics and trade gossip. It involves close observation of competitors to learn where they are strong and where they are weak. Understanding your competition is an important element of examining the external influences and environment of your business. From a strategic perspective CI is vital. These are the questions you should be asking: Who is the competition now? Who might it be five years from now? What are the strategies, objectives, and goals of my major competitors? What is the performance record of my competitors? Specifically, what is their sales growth, market share, and profitability? How important is each target market to my competitors? How satisfied do my competitors appear with their performance? What is their level of commitment to each of these markets? What are the strengths and limitations of my competitors? What weaknesses make my competitors vulnerable? What strategic changes are my competitors likely to make? What effects might these have on my strategy?

Companies such as Telus, Crystal Decisions, Pivotal Software, Intrawest, and Future Shop are all actively involved in CI practices. Jeff Crowter, director of marketing operations at Telus, heads a team of individuals who devote their sole efforts to obtaining information and strategically using it to keep the company on the leading edge of a fiercely competitive marketplace. CI is a centralized function of marketing and corporate development at Telus, but, stresses Jeff, "We rely not only on our department but all employees for the collection of CI information. We also openly share much of this information through a company intranet portal, so all departments can benefit." There are three general sources for CI information: what competitors say about themselves, what others say about them, and what you are able to gather through your research efforts. There are a number of techniques to keep tabs on your competition.

1. Look at published materials and public documents. Examples include financial reports, annual reports, speeches, websites, newspaper and magazine articles, books, and TV or radio interviews. Clipping services can be hired to scan articles in the media concerning designated competitors. Many business publications make back issue articles searchable online for easy access. Job postings on a website or career ads may indicate competitor intentions and planned strategies. If your competition is a publicly traded company, buy some shares so you receive shareholder information. Analyze their financial statements. 80 to 90% of all CI information is public knowledge. You just need to use journalistic skills to take one fact and follow it through to get the critical pieces of information.

2. Source information from government agencies under the Freedom of Information Act. Licence applications and agreements with provincial and municipal governments may indicate future intentions of competitors.

3. Observe competitors or analyze physical evidence. Visit your competitors' operations and evaluate service and product offerings. Buy competitor products and tear them apart. Analyze manufacturing methods and production costs.

4. Conduct a company profile. Look at your competitors' financial situation, technology, workforce, facilities, capabilities, supply and distribution chain, management strengths, key executives, strategic alliances, and positioning strategy. You need to know as much about these competitive factors as you can.

5. Do a personality profile of key personnel at competing companies. Look at recent changes in staffing. Past successes, failures, strengths, weaknesses, mentors, and associates may indicate future strategies or competitive styles.

6. Talk to recruits or employees of competing companies. Often unrewarded employees are anxious to impress. This can be done in job interviews or at trade show networking. Let ethical behaviour be your guide. You must not overtly ask pointed questions of a competitive nature, but you can certainly listen.

7. Talk to your competitors' customers. Again, ethics should guide your behaviour.

8. Conduct personal interviews. This can be one of the best techniques. You should approach this with the intention of learning something, but with the willingness to give some information back that can be shared. This will ensure your source doesn't feel exploited and will keep the line of contact open for the future.

Noticeably absent from this list is the "dumpster diving" technique of looking through your competitors' trash or the practice of luring key competitors' management through recruitment with the aim of obtaining trade secrets and insider knowledge. "Ethical collection is the only way to ensure good business practices over the long term," says Derek Thompson, senior associate with Ibis Research, a company specializing in business intelligence and knowledge management. "Data collected through questionable ethics invariably will catch up with you. The resulting negative media coverage or worse, legal action, will have damaging effects." Once you have accumulated information, you can start to turn it into knowledge and strategy through analysis. The management model "Porters Five Forces" provides a solid framework to classify your information. It incorporates the areas of potential new entrants, substitute products/services, power of suppliers, power of buyers, and the influence of technology, demographics, economy, and government regulations.

Although not critical for the small business owner, large corporations with teams devoted to CI might consider investing in software analysis tools. Derek Thompson notes that business intelligence software is data collection and management focused at the moment. He suggests referring to the Fuld and Co. website (www.fuld.com) for a detailed review of intelligence software products. Fuld and Co. is a Cambridge, Massachusetts-based world leader in competitive intelligence. However, your existing word processing, spreadsheet, and database software might be all you need to build a list of contacts and store data on competitors. Remember that software is a tool. Your program will only be as good as the human-source intelligence it is built on. You may wish to solicit the assistance of an outside organization. Marketing research firms or business intelligence and knowledge management companies engage in different forms of CI. The benefit here is in the expert data collection and analysis. The Canadian Business Intelligence Association (www.cbia.ca), the Society of Competitive Intelligence Professionals (www.scip.org) and the Professional Marketing Research Society (www.pmrs-aprm.com) are all good sources for professional assistance.

In today's competitive environment, to ignore your competition is to do so at your own peril. From a strategic perspective, competitive intelligence is vital to your company's success.

A note to readers: The Professional Marketing Research Society (PMRS) is now known as the Marketing and Research Intelligence Association (MRIA). Visit their website at www.mria-arim.ca for more information.

CHAPTER 8

Sales

■ ■ ■

Nothing happens until someone buys something. Think about it. Everything you do, all the goals you work toward in marketing lead to one thing: the sale. Whether you are marketing your company's services, products, or yourself, you should learn how to sell! Selling is a skill set and it can be learned. The more businesses understand about the psychology of buying, the better they'll be at marketing and selling. It's that simple.

Simple Sales Tips from a Successful Five-Year-Old

■ ■ ■

Business in Vancouver newspaper, August 26, 2003

It's amazing how some small businesses and even major corporations often misunderstand strategic marketing and sales. More amazing perhaps is that a lesson in the basics could be had at the hands of a young child.

My five-year-old son recently made $15 in one and a half hours selling lemonade on the West Vancouver seawall. He set up his stand in a high pedestrian traffic location along the seawall at the bottom of 19th Street, a natural start or end for a walk and a high traffic intersection. It was a shaded area with a view well away from any restaurants, water fountains, or vending machines.

Lesson #1: Location matters. Be easily accessible to as many of your target customers as you can. Make the environment pleasant. Distance yourself from competitors. He placed a large sign - Alex and Pat's homemade lemonade 25¢ - on a red-draped table. He then placed signs fifteen metres on either side along the seawall telling people that lemonade was just ahead.

Lesson #2: Advertise your product or service. Customers need to know you exist. Tease them with your ads. Tell them why you're better. My son didn't just stand there. He walked around and invited customers to stop. He pointed people to his stand and with a big smile he asked if they wanted some lemonade. He'd use the assumptive close, "Gee, it's a hot day - I'll bet you'd like a lemonade to cool off." He pre-qualified his customers. Noting that more women seemed to buy and in particular, women with strollers, he would select them in advance as they approached and extend a personal invitation. He accepted prepayment. His response to someone who said they had a water bottle was, "That's okay - you can pay now and have a lemonade when you come back!" They did, and he had cash in hand. He made two-for-one offers. When two people had only a quarter between them, he gave the second drink for free, but not before reminding them that the next time he was there, they could buy more. He suggested to one man that he still looked thirsty and perhaps he needed another. The customer bought a second glass. His clean white shirt was tucked in and his hands and face were spotless. He worked in a team with his sister behind the table while he directed traffic to the stand.

Lesson #3: Personal selling is very effective. Work the crowd. Meet your customers. Present yourself well. Be upbeat. Pre-qualify your target group. Up-sell if you can. Use the assumptive close. Make special offers to get future sales. Sell as a team to support business. Learn that prepayment is good. Make sure your product is superior. The product he sold was homemade with fresh lemons, served cold with ice in a big glass. It tasted good.

Lesson #4: You might get away once with great marketing and a crappy product, but only an excellent experience will bring customers back. He sold the lemonade for 25¢ a glass. This was certainly a bargain compared to Starbucks up the street, but since it was homemade and the product costs were low, he still had a decent margin. Plus, his supplier, his mom, didn't charge him for the goods. Several people paid him more than 25¢.

Lesson #5: Price your product based on your costs, your desired margins, and the prices charged by your competitors. People may pay more than asked when you're five and cute, but don't count on it later in life.

Lesson #6: Know the laws and regulations affecting your business and industry. Don't trust your mother. I suspect there was a bylaw prohibiting the sale of product in a public space such as the seawall without a licence. Common sense would dictate that this would likely be loosely interpreted for a five-year-old and a one-off afternoon business venture. However, as you get older, the law is likely to be less lenient.

There you have it. Some basic rules for marketing and selling your products and services from a five-year-old. Simple, isn't it?

Sales Lessons from the Long, Winding Road

■ ■ ■

Business in Vancouver newspaper, May 2, 2006

Dear Mr. Sales Rep:

A friend of mine drives a twenty-year-old car. It's not because she can't afford a new one - she just hates the car-buying experience. I assured her that the sales process had become a lot more sophisticated. I too am shopping for an economical second family vehicle. In fact, I went shopping with my two kids recently. I didn't exactly run screaming from your dealership, but I certainly had to resist on several occasions the desire to teach you about sales. Mind if I share our experience? The sales and marketing universe will thank you.

Lesson #1: Rapport building is important. The more you know about me, the more you know about how to sell to me. Engage in dialogue and break the ice. Start to tap into what matters to me. I have emotional triggers, and unless you build rapport, you'll never find out what they are. If you are going to call me by name, make sure it's mine. Better, ask me my name before you spend forty-five minutes with me. And while you're at it, introduce yourself. I might want to remember you when I come back to purchase.

Lesson #2: Know your competitive environment. You must be able to position your product compared to competitors and show the benefits. I shouldn't have to beg you for competitor comparatives. You've been asked this question before and you'll be asked it again. Prepare and position yourself. It is your job to know both your product and your competitors' inside out.

Lesson #3: Observe and listen intently. Ask lots of questions. Don't draw hasty conclusions from observation, but use them as a clue for further probing. My questions are important, and if you listen, you will realize I am telling you how I want to be sold. I will tell you what is important to me and what isn't. Don't start selling until you can show me features that are relevant. I will tell you my absolute criteria. I will tell you about my lifestyle. I drove up in a Volvo with two kids. Safety is important to me. That front seat air bag sensor might have been a good feature to show me.

Lesson #4: You must have sales materials to give away. Your sales kit is your tool. A builder wouldn't build without a hammer. You can't sell without your sales tools. I don't really care if you've run out of sales brochures - fix the problem. Pull some material off the web. Get more printed. I am on a research mission. I want to leave with information to help make my decision. If you rely on me to look it up on the web when I get home, I may just stop at a competitor and forget to get your sales information.

Lesson #5: Up-sell me if you can. That's your job. But push at your peril. If you think after probing my criteria that I am making a mistake to not consider a better feature, tell me. Save me from myself. If you're right, I will respect you. However, if I tell you repeatedly I do not want something, please stop. I don't need the feature. I don't want to pay for it. And I certainly don't want to give you the increased commission on it.

Lesson #6: Realize that if a woman sets foot on a car lot, she is there because she wants to buy a car. She may or may not want to buy your car. And she won't be buying today if you've never met her before, so get over it. Women don't kick tires, they do research. I was gathering information about your car and about you. I was testing you. How do you think you did? Please don't ask if I'm going to buy today. I'll tell you when I'm ready. You hadn't answered all my questions yet and there was no rapport. I liked your car, but you were too pushy. Yes, I was the decision-maker, I just wasn't deciding today.

You were polite and you represented a great product, but you just didn't do your job very well. Good sales techniques are at the root of all commerce. Nothing happens in this world until someone sells something. So isn't it worth learning how to do it right?

Sincerely,
Mary Charleson

Speak Up: It Could Be Your Best Marketing Move

. . .

Business in Vancouver newspaper, August 24, 2005

It's inevitable in business. You are at a function and someone asks you to stand up and tell people about what you do. Alternatively, you're asked to make a presentation to an influential group of investors or colleagues. Instead of sheer panic pumping through your veins, wouldn't it be nice if you rose and greeted the request as a terrific opportunity to position yourself, your business, and your knowledge? You can spend much time plotting your marketing strategy, but the shameful truth is that you, and your capacity to speak with knowledge, honesty, and wit about your business, products, or services are the single most powerful tool in your personal marketing arsenal. If this is beyond your comfort zone, make a commitment now to improve your public speaking abilities. You need to get those butterflies flying in formation.

I'm not talking about learning the latest presentation skills or how to use the wizardry of PowerPoint or Keynote for audiovisuals. In fact, we've likely all sat through too many content-laden presentations where someone relied heavily on technology and read to us painfully exactly what was on-screen. All this frequently followed a charade of fault-filled test runs with unfamiliar technology. Instead, what I'm talking about is learning the skills of a great orator, becoming someone who can tell a compelling story, evoke emotion, and persuade with power. Someone who can use the power of words to command an audience and keep technology, as a support mechanism, in its place. That someone should be you. This learned skill could be the single most valuable tool in your personal and professional positioning strategy. This is where marketing gets personal. Whether it's a two-minute introduction or a one-hour presentation, here are some pointers. Accomplished leaders know the power of a well-told story. They take listeners on a journey. They don't just discharge facts and data. To tell an authoritative story, they establish a communication objective and construct their presentation with an outcome in mind. Is your objective to persuade, inform, or inspire? Craft your story with a clear objective in mind.

Context is important. A presentation requires context and background to be meaningful. Without it, your persuasive sales pitch or inspiration to action will fall short later in the talk. Relate your key points back to context. Leaders know the power of influence that comes with great context. And please, research your audience. Do not talk up or down to them.

Be personable. People become engaged with those whom they feel close to. Good speakers make you feel that they are interacting with you as an individual. They make eye contact. They interact with their audience and move throughout the room. They customize their material for the audience by taking the time to research the group.

Never, ever rush a presentation. If you run short of time cut out material. If you know you will be speaking after several others, count on the possibility of being cut short. Plan for it. Prepare different-length versions of your talk. Learn that pauses are good. They provide space around words and help drive home a well-made point. Silence can be golden if used well.

Talk slowly, project your voice, make eye contact, and use gestures. Many novice speakers talk far too quickly at first. Experienced speakers do the reverse. They start slowly and then speed up when content demands it. Speak not only with your voice but with your body.

Use technology as a tool, not a crutch. The higher up the corporate food chain, the fewer tools like PowerPoint are used. This is for a good reason. These people are usually better speakers. Audiovisuals should complement, not replicate your presentation. Make sure your talk can stand on its own and then use AV to make it even stronger. Well-chosen words, delivered in a powerful manner, will eclipse a glitzy presentation. Did some of history's best orators, like Trudeau or Churchill, have PowerPoint? Exactly.

Always have a rehearsed two-minute pitch about your business ready. You never know when you might be able to use it. You need to make that short period of time work for you. There are many organizations and companies that can help you become a better speaker, but one of the best is Toastmasters International. There's also CAPS, the Canadian Association of Professional Speakers. To find a club in your area visit www.toastmasters.org or www.canadianspeakers.org and click the links to search for clubs in your vicinity. Make this the year you commit to improving your speaking abilities. It may be the best marketing move you make.

Full Sale: Marketing's Seafaring Similarities

■ ■ ■

Business in Vancouver newspaper, October 26, 2004

I was fortunate to spend the last glorious sunny week of September sailing with my family on BC's coastal waters. Although I had promised to park my brain for a few days and not think about work, I found myself considering the parallels between sailing and marketing. Even landlubbers will be able to appreciate what sailing has to teach us.

1. You can never have too much information. When sailing it's best to have all implements of assistance at hand: charts, compass, GPS, and cruising guides. Because your very survival hinges on staying clear of rocks, knowing where you are at all times is a necessity. The more information the better. This is much like your marketing strategy. You need internal information on your capabilities, strengths, and weaknesses, and external market information on competitors, changing markets or new technologies, and regulations that are apt to affect your industry. Information is king. You need lots of it to stay off the rocks.

2. Despite the number of crew on board, there is only one skipper. On a boat someone has to take charge, accept final responsibility, and lead the group. Although it is possible to have several talented and knowledgeable people on board, only one can lead. The very safety of the crew and the ability to make your

final destination depends on it. This is not unlike the CEO or the marketing manager. Those at the top must show strong leadership and staff must follow their direction. Of course, it helps if the skipper has gained the crew's respect through a demonstration of knowledge and experience. Ditto in business.

3. Never leave port without a plan. Before pulling the anchor or departing the dock, you should know where you are going and how long it will take to get there. You also need to consider the wind, tide, and weather conditions, and have a backup plan should the wind or weather change or you experience a mechanical failure. These are all critical considerations for boaters. Likewise in marketing, you need to define goals for your product, service, or business. You need to know where you're going. You need to have an estimate for how long it will take to achieve these goals and the checkpoints for success along the way. You need to consider all internal and external forces such as competitors, knock-off products, changes in technology, changed cost structures in your business, or employee capabilities. These are like safety maintenance of your boat or considering the influences of weather. All must be factored in when making your marketing plan.

4. Alert all crew before changing directions with your sails. On a boat, nothing is more dangerous than a quick, ill-planned tack or jibe. It's hard on the boat, and worse, can threaten the very safety of the crew or that of other boats in proximity. All crew must be alerted to the planned change, and they must act as a team to execute their role completing a safe and quick change of direction. This is not unlike the employees in your business. Everyone must be on board for a planned change in marketing. Customers, like the other boats, must be considered and informed. All staff must be aware of the role they play and how they will work together to execute a change in strategy.

5. Know the forecast before setting anchor. When picking an anchorage, sailors must be aware of water depth, tide changes while they plan to be there, current and possible changes to wind direction, the location of other boats and their anticipated swing. This is not unlike forecasting in marketing. Before setting your anchor and committing to a plan and strategy, all influences must be considered. At this point it comes full circle back to constantly collecting information. Be aware of your industry and make competitive intelligence a priority.

The beauty of sailing is that it demands skill, knowledge, alertness, and planning. There is nothing more invigorating than a day on the high seas. Business too can deliver these same pleasures. But as any good sailor knows, to be good you must be prepared to constantly learn. This credo also applies to business.

For Success Stories, Starting at the Ground Floor, Ready Your Elevator Pitch

■ ■ ■

Business in Vancouver newspaper, August 24, 2004

Society suffers from communications overload. From the moment we wake until our head hits the pillow again, we're inundated with messages and information. Much of it has to do with marketing and advertising, and only a fraction of what was originally communicated is retained. Our only defence is to keep it simple. We remember only what is of interest and easily understood. How then do you position your business and communicate to cut through the clutter? How do you become the fraction of information that is retained? You keep it simple. In communication, less is often more. This philosophy works well for business positioning and marketing efforts. Do you have an elevator pitch? Suppose a person critical to the future success of your business stepped into the elevator with you one day. Fate having delivered you a few moments to position your business, what would you say? This is not unlike the fraction of time you have to position your business in the mind of the consumer. In one brief sentence you should be able to define what you do, how you're different from competitors, and why anyone should care. And if you define yourself by how you make a difference in your customers' lives and not by what you sell, you can create a powerful emotional connection with them.

Let's look at a few examples: Quiznos is one of the fastest-growing sandwich restaurants in North America. With over 1,200 locations, they have opened numerous stores in the Lower Mainland in recent years. Their sub sandwiches are toasted on artisan breads using fresh ingredients and original sauces. The upscale sandwich is positioned for busy consumers looking for a fresh alternative to traditional fast food. The "toasted tastes better" advertising message positions them simply and directly against their primary competitor, Subway. Marketing messages tell customers what to expect, how Quiznos is different, and most importantly, what's in it for them. It is not easy to enter a market as a latecomer in a category and then compete with industry leader Subway, but Quiznos has done a good job of positioning their message in a simple manner.

Fido, the digital wireless service offered by Microcell Solutions, was launched in 1996. They revolutionized the wireless industry with a simple approach to pricing and contracts. They had one package price and no contract was required. In the face of complex rate plans and lengthy contracts offered by competitors, they positioned themselves as friendly and easy to understand. Consumers clearly understood what was in it for them. Fido has consistently reinforced this position with catchy advertising campaigns. City Fido is their latest product entry and in keeping with their positioning of simplicity. City Fido offers unlimited local calls and targets consumers who want to abandon their residential landline service. Aimed primarily at youth and singles, the ad shows a pile of discarded home phones. It conveys a clear and memorable message. I recently guest lectured for Capilano College's Arts and Entertainment Management Program. When I asked the class of twenty-three how many had only a cell phone and no home phone, seven put up their hands. That's a whopping 30%. Anecdotal data to be sure, but an indication that the potential for growth in this category is there for the taking. Although Telus has now packaged a similar offering, they haven't succeeded in communicating the attributes and product positioning in the simple manner that Fido did.

The airline industry is a tough, competitive environment, yet Westjet, a low-cost carrier, is one of the most successful airlines in Canadian history. Their position is simple, yet it distinguishes them strongly against competitors. They offer low-cost fares, and they deliver service with a genuine smile and sense of humour. All advertising and communications reinforces this position.

So the next time that elevator door opens, do you know what you're going to say? Better yet, don't wait for the elevator. Your potential customers want to hear your pitch right now. Think like a customer. Tell them how you'll make a difference in their lives. Select that one specific concept to hang your hat on. Then make sure your actions and all marketing and advertising reinforce this position. It's the only way to cut through the customer's wall of indifference. It can be that simple.

Four Currencies Add Up to Better Business Results

■ ■ ■

Business in Vancouver newspaper, July 29, 2003

Savvy marketers recognize that customers are influenced by several currencies beyond money. A currency is anything of value to the customer: money, time, security, and feeling special. There are many ways to compete for loyalty when your marketing strategy views customers from this perspective. To create value you must deliver on as many of these four currencies as you can. Value can be delivered at the financial, functional, or emotional level.

Let's look at how to leverage each currency and see how some local businesses have built a successful strategy doing it.

1. Money: We're all familiar with the currency of money. There are two ways to create monetary value; either offer the customer the best price or make them believe the price they are paying is a fair exchange for superior value. To use this currency effectively you must understand the emotional and functional values of your target customers.

Dayton Boot Co. successfully sells superior value at a premium price. Since 1946 they have made handcrafted and custom order work, casual, and motorcycle boots in Vancouver. Dayton boasts Hollywood stars as some of their loyal customers. People who buy their boots place value in quality and craftsmanship and they're willing to pay for it. The premium price is justified in the mind of the customer.

Discount bookseller Book Warehouse offers customers cheap prices on books. The best price position is a trade-off for less depth in subject selections. Saving money on book purchases is the primary motivator in the mind of their customer.

2. Time: For some time is more valuable than money. Others will willingly exchange their time to save money. To use time effectively, you must understand the value trade-off your customers are willing to place on it. As with the currency of money, the value of time for individual customers will vary for different products and services. The challenge is to recognize when it can be leveraged to your advantage.

Ikea has built a successful strategy based on the concept that some consumers are willing to exchange their time to save money. Most furnishings are mass-produced and packed flat for delivery and assembly by customers. The time to assemble and deliver goods has been transferred to the consumer, which allows a labour cost savings reflected in the price of goods.

If you've ever spent time searching a dazzling array of paint chips and collecting sample tins in a quest for the perfect colour, you'll appreciate the simplicity and time-saving approach presented at Restoration Hardware. They sell only eleven colours of paint. Each is selected based on current design trends and all colours work together. A complicated, time-consuming process has been made simple and quick. For their target consumer, the premium paid for colour pre-selection is worth the time saved.

3. Security: Security is all about feeling safe. This is where buying behaviour is influenced by perceptions. To use this currency effectively you must understand the values and motivations of your target customers. Although physical security can be a primary motivator for the purchase of such items as alarm systems or cell phones, the desire to feel safe has a much greater reach. It is an influence that can be used to justify or take chances on a purchase. Everyone wants to feel they've done the right thing. The more your business can offer and even guarantee the feeling of being safe, the more successful your strategy. Businesses with a "no questions asked" return policy, free trials, or a price guarantee all offer security. Capers Community Markets offer customers a money-back guarantee on anything in their store. Because many items they sell are things their customers may not have tried before, they want people to feel comfortable experimenting. The guarantee offers purchase security. Shoppers Drug Mart also has a "no questions asked" return policy on all of its cosmetics. Customers feel safe trying out a new product that may or may not work for them after several weeks' trial at home.

4. Feeling special: By creating that special connection with the customer, making them feel valued, good about themselves, or happy that your business solved a problem for them, you will make them feel special. Customers' needs and wants are heavily influenced by the desire to feel special. To use this currency effectively you should strive to fully understand your customer on many levels and then use this knowledge to deliver products and services that cause them to form an emotional bond with your business. Deliver on this one and there will be a lot more money currency coming your way. When Rocky Mountaineer guests disembark the train for the night and take the motor coach to their hotel, they find their luggage waiting in their room upon arrival. Anticipating customer needs and having a desire to exceed expectations, the company delivers the luggage in advance by truck. This expedited service costs them $200,000 a year but contributes to a memorable experience. Guests feel special.

Any one of the four currencies - money, time, security, and feeling special, can be the dominant motivation for your customers.

Money is usually the primary currency. The remaining three will play a supporting role in justifying their buying decision. Your marketing strategy should address all your customers' currencies to truly deliver value and allow you to be perceived as superior to your competitors.

Trends

■ ■ ■

I'm a big believer in research. That's one of the reasons I have worked closely with Pollara, a Canadian polling firm, and TNS Canadian Facts, one of Canada's largest and most respected marketing and social research organizations. It is critical to have a pulse on the market. It can help you measure what's going on and, even more importantly, gauge what trends are emerging. This section reveals some articles based on research and highlights some trends that I've spotted, but you'll note that research is frequently quoted in articles throughout this book.

This chapter begins with some observations on the credit and financial crisis that became prominent in October of 2008. I offer some observations on trends likely to unfold in marketing and communications as this crisis plays out.

Big Ideas About Thinking Small in an Era of Consumer Uncertainty

. . .

Business in Vancouver newspaper, October 21, 2008

Things have gone from bad to worse south of the border. The endless stream of financial turmoil makes one want to run for cover with a good bottle of scotch. While consumption is not widely considered a wise financial move, it could certainly dull the economic pain of late. So what might all this mean for those of us who make our living ensuring consumers continue to spend? Likely a slowdown. You'd have to be delusional to think that the US, as Canada's largest trading partner, could go down the toilet and we wouldn't at least feel a pull from the current. With that in mind, I predict five themes to emerge in marketing this quarter and throughout the coming year:

1. A backlash against anything big and corporate. Main Street America is furious with the CEOs, banks, and investment houses that got them into this mess. While Main Street can't lay blame for the additional self-inflicted consumer debt load, they'll try. For the next while, big will be bad. Now is the time to think small. Patronizing local business will become fashionable as people seek to support those in their own community. Companies with a social strategy that supports the community will fare better.

2. A sentiment of anti-consumerism. The ground has shifted and companies that push product blatantly will experience a backlash.

This could make for some interesting 2008 Christmas advertising.
3. Value of life's precious moments. Think family, friends, and experiences. Out with material possessions, in with the warm and fuzzy. Marketers who key in on this sentiment will be better positioned in the coming months.

4. Low-cost and high-value offerings. When times get tougher people become price conscious. Suddenly thrift will be fashionable. If you're in the luxury market, perceived value and exceptional service will become increasingly important.

5. Humour and escapism as themes. When it all gets too serious, companies that can entertain and make people laugh with their messages will benefit. While big expenditures will be less in vogue for many, people will pay for small pleasures in a quest for a temporary escape.

Let's take a look closer look at one of those trends: the backlash against anything big and corporate. For the next while, anyone who has seemed to profit at the expense of Main Street will be under scrutiny. As the entire financial crisis unravels in the US, consumers will turn to smaller local companies, ones they feel they can trust.

Local businesses and those that support the community they function in will do well. Vancity has just relaunched their Jumpstart high-interest savings account. In addition to paying a higher than average return, the account funnels a percent of profits back into the Futures Foundation to help fight poverty. The Futures Foundation helps low-income families by offering money management skills and asset management to create financial self-sufficiency in their communities. TV, transit, direct mail, and online efforts launched the first week of October. The time is right for a safe place to park money in the storm while earning a higher than average return. Let's face it: anything on the positive side of the ledger would be welcome these days. And the philanthropic community-based component is well aligned for this trend. Vancity, with their triple bottom line of financial, social, and environmental returns, is a great example of a company supporting the communities they do business in. The Jumpstart account is yet another extension of this approach. They should weather the backlash against anything big and corporate, although they may have to convince some people that any bank or credit union is safer than under their mattress these days!

So as David Ogilvy, Madison Avenue advertising agency legend, said in his 1959 Volkswagen ad, think small. Patronizing local businesses will become fashionable as people seek to support those who give back to their own community.

Sins, Staples, and Small Pleasures on Consumer Wish Lists

■ ■ ■

Business in Vancouver newspaper, November 24, 2008

It's official south of the border, and likely to touch down here at some point in the future. The "R-word" has landed. In recessions our purchase habits go astray. In an economy built on buying stuff, receding purchase habits can cause havoc, especially an economy where many purchases straddle the line between unnecessary and completely unnecessary. The trick for marketers is to acknowledge where consumers might be at, while not sending them into panic. The best recession campaigns won't mention the economy. They'll entertain, humour, empower, and make people feel normal, while reserving an undercurrent that things aren't exactly normal.

Last month I predicted five themes that would emerge in marketing with a depressed economy. I received a lot of feedback, so this month we'll dig a little deeper on the subject. A review of the five trends:

1. A backlash against anything big and corporate.
2. A sentiment of anti-consumerism.
3. Value of life's precious moments.
4. Low-cost and high-value offerings.
5. Humour and escapism as themes.

While big expenditures will be less in vogue for many, people will always pay for *sins, staples,* and *small pleasures* in a quest for an escape. Sins are those things like alcohol, chocolate, lottery tickets, tobacco, and other items that they could cut out, but won't sacrifice easily. Staples are food, household cleaning and personal care items, shelter, and basic transportation. Small pleasures are the things that make you feel decadent while not breaking bank. Think $1 loonie lattes (do they exist? they should!), $20 family movie nights, pedicures, clothing accessories (rather than buying the whole new outfit), haircuts, keeping in touch with family and friends, etc. Sins, staples, and small pleasures are fairly recession proof. They will be the secret to marketing in a tougher economy.

But what if you're not in the sins, staples, and small pleasures business? Anyone can take advantage of these areas; you just need to rethink the way you market. One company doing this is Aeroplan. Having recently gone public and no longer being linked to Air Canada, their new branded tag line is now simply "Rewarding life." With four million members, 93% of whom are in Canada, and 22% penetration of Canadian households, their rewards-based loyalty program is all about adding small pleasures to life. They have gone well beyond air travel and accommodation as rewards to offer everyday items such as TVs, iPods, entertainment tickets, cameras, bikes, appliances, and a whole lot more. But here's where it gets interesting. They are tying the earning of *small pleasures* into the purchase of *staples*. An agreement with Sobey's groceries has put this in place. You can buy a necessary item such as food and earn points toward a small pleasure such as an iPod for free through their association with Aeroplan rewards. It's a brilliant move in recessionary times. The whole notion of travel and material goods as rewards offers "escapism" and "value in life's precious moments" while being delivered through small pleasures, which ties back nicely to the five trends. Might there be a small pleasure angle to your business?

A note to readers: In 2009 Canada officially entered a recession, along with many other countries. What initially appeared to be an American debt and bad lending problem quickly spread as it became ever apparent that lending practices had linked the economies of many countries worldwide. Although we're told that Canada's conservative banking practices have made things better here, consumer sentiment has been impacted. Canadian companies now must understand this new mood and position their businesses accordingly.

Credit Card Call Highlights Consumer Vulnerability

■ ■ ■

Business in Vancouver newspaper, February 5, 2008

"Good morning Mrs. Charleson. This is Tammy from Mosaic MasterCard security office calling. This call is being recorded for legal purposes. We have reason to believe the security on your credit card has been compromised. May I speak to you about purchases billed to your card the last couple of days?"

That's the beginning of a call I received last week. MasterCard had obviously tracked purchase patterns and realized that something might be amiss when they saw that I had apparently purchased a computer in Australia, followed by numerous small online Yahoo Wallet transactions and then an attempt to buy a car in India. There were several legitimate transactions actually made by me within this four-day time period, but the notable switch to numerous online purchases daily caused a flag. I suspect the car purchase in India made it a slamdunk!

As reassuring as it may be to know they monitored and caught the problem within four days and will not hold me accountable for the transactions, it is alarming to realize how vulnerable a consumer can be. In a subsequent discussion with them I learned that they believed an online compromise was unlikely, and that it was more likely a case of an unsophisticated fraudulent attempt to generate random account and expiry numbers with no name attached to find a combination that worked with an online retailer. The perpetrator, likely thousands of miles away, may well still be randomly generating number combinations daily in hopes of hitting the jackpot. Although credit card companies are reluctant to lower credit limits, I have now made a conscious decision to maintain one card with a low credit limit for exclusive use when making online purchases. The next time they might not be as quick to catch the fraud, or as generous with erasing the transactions. I'm taking no chances.

Is this type of scare apt to put Canadians off making online purchases in the future? Not likely. In fact it would appear we're one of the most e-commerce and social network savvy countries in the world. In a recent Statistics Canada survey, 71% of Vancouverites reported using the Internet. Two-thirds of us use it every day. While 57% of users went online to browse and do research, 43% engaged in commerce to buy goods or services. Almost three-quarters of respondents said they were concerned (33%) or very concerned (40%) about privacy and security, and more than half (57%) were concerned about Internet credit card use.

TNS Canadian Facts recently published a study of Canadians on social networking and blog usage. The poll found that online teens and young adults were the heaviest users of social networking sites, with 83% of the thirteen-to-seventeen-year-olds and 74% of eighteen-to-twenty-nine-year-olds having visited at least one such site. Not surprisingly, older people were less likely to have spent any time on sites such as Facebook and MySpace, but the incidence was still quite high among middle-aged and older Canadians. Sixty percent of people in their thirties had visited at least one social networking site and 45% of those in their forties had done so. Among those over fifty, 33% claimed to have visited such a site. Considering Facebook and MySpace have only burst on to the scene recently, it is quite remarkable that 53% of Canadians overall claimed to have visited a social networking site.

In November 2007 it was reported that Microsoft had acquired ownership in Facebook. Speculation at the time was that they were developing software to mine users' personal data to be able to serve up targeted advertising. While Google and Yahoo had been using profiling of customer search topics to serve up advertising, the use of social networking data was a new twist. Recently Facebook launched "SocialAds," which can be tagged onto member activities such as reviewing or buying products and then shared with Facebook users' networks. Publishers such as Random House have placed flyer campaigns for book event promotions with great success through this medium. These Web 2.0 applications hold amazing potential and are delivering real measurable results right now.

Social networking sites are a moving target, however, and what's hot today may not be tomorrow. Canadians are heavy users but guard their identity and security closely. Just ask Tammy at MasterCard.

Marketing Financial Services Offers Host of 21st-Century Opportunities

■ ■ ■

Business in Vancouver newspaper, November 21, 2007

The successful marketing of financial services, investments, and insurance is an area likely to get a great deal more attention as the baby boomer bubble moves through the ages of fifty to seventy years. Although some institutions are firmly entrenched in historical views of this group, particularly concerning the ways to appeal to women, most have at least realized that there is a tremendous opportunity if they get it right.

In October, my company worked with TNS Canadian Facts to survey 1,200 people across Canada on the subject of financial services. We were interested in customer satisfaction, levels of investment research, decision-making responsibility, and preferences in dealing with financial advisors. In this article I consider baby boomer responses in particular, since the results hold some key insights to marketing to this group.

Satisfaction with primary financial institution: Generally the older the respondent the more satisfied they were. Since wealth usually accumulates with age, this is good news for financial institutions. Overall, 64% of Canadians and 70% of those over the age of fifty were quite satisfied. However, that still leaves a dubious 30% of those over fifty wanting improvements. Take note:

that could be a lot of wealth looking for a new home.

Frequency of doing your own research when making investment decisions: Overall, 52% of men and 47% of women said they always or frequently did their own research. Young women eighteen to twenty-four and older women over seventy did the least amount of their own research. Only 36% of this group reported always or frequently doing it themselves. 28% of both men and women aged fifty to sixty-nine said they seldom or never did their own research. And 42% of women over seventy reported seldom or never doing their own investment research. Since there is a lot of wealth both accumulated and strategically dispersed after fifty, there is a big opportunity gap for research and advice to this group. This is particularly acute for women over seventy, who are likely to live well into their late eighties or early nineties.

Whether they are the *sole* decision-maker of finances and investments: Generally those eighteen to twenty-four and those over sixty-five were more likely to be making decisions on their own, primarily because these are the age groups most likely to be single. 58% of women and 59% of men fifty to sixty-nine reported being the sole decision-maker, while 70% of both men and women over seventy years reported being the sole decision-maker for finances and investments.

Whether they are the *key* decision-maker of finances and investments for their spouse: Generally men were more likely to perceive themselves as the key decision-maker. 56% of males fifty to sixty-nine and 77% of males over seventy years of age said they were the key decision-maker for their spouse. However, 51% of females fifty to sixty-nine and 66% of females over seventy years also reported being the key decision-maker for their spouse. Perception is only part of reality, it appears.

Preference of dealing with a financial services advisor: Although gender and age didn't matter for the majority of people, for the 20% of the population who had some preference, generally age trumps youth and women trump men. While the preference for both older male and older female advisors was the strongest, older females were the most preferred. 15% of males and 10% of females eighteen to twenty-four preferred older women advisors. 17% of women over fifty also preferred older female advisors. Although young female advisors were preferred by 17% of males eighteen to twenty-four, the preference fell to 1% for women over fifty. Young male advisors were the least preferred overall. "Older advisors certainly seem to have an edge," notes Raymond Gee, senior research associate at TNS Canadian Facts, "but competence appears to be key." Well guys, it might be time to dye those temples grey. And if you want to connect with baby boomer women, hire an experienced woman.

These insights start to provide a view into the touchpoints for baby boomer investors. As newly minted Vancity CEO Tamara Vrooman recently noted in the media, "There will be an unprecedented transfer of wealth as baby boomers age." Banks, brokers, and investment advisors need to get it right. Marketing their services properly to this group represents a huge opportunity.

Poll Surveys Consumer Views on Income and Debt

■ ■ ■

Business in Vancouver newspaper, February 7, 2006

A note to readers: I offer this article for its historical perspective. I invite you to read it and reflect on what it means, now viewed from the perspective of an economy that has since entered a recession. Might there have been a hint of things to come?

The need for marketers to monitor consumers' incomes and their attitudes toward savings is becoming increasingly critical because the scale of consumer debt has made millions of households vulnerable to shocks in the economy. In Vancouver, we enjoy a bullish attitude toward the economy but we are also under large debt burdens when it comes to housing. To further understand consumer attitudes and the possible implications for marketers, I undertook a study with Pollara, a Canadian national public opinion and market research firm. We asked people:

1. Are you making more money now than you did five years ago?
2. Are you saving more money now that you did five years ago?
3. Do you carry more debt now than you did five years ago?
4. Do you feel financially more secure than you did five years ago?
5. If interest rates increased by 2%, would you be in trouble?

Of course, perception is not always reality, so caution is prudent in the interpretation of results.

On income: Incremental increases in income seem to get smaller with age. Those with higher education experienced greater increases in income. Those with higher incomes had a greater likelihood of continuing an income increase. However, there was a striking difference between male and female responses. 74% of males eighteen to thirty-five felt very strongly that they were making more money than they did five years ago, while only 66% of women eighteen to thirty-five felt that way. This perceived income discrepancy between males and females remained consistent through all age groups.

On savings: The ability to save has little reflection on what has been earned. "A lot of professional people and high-income earners get into trouble. They spend more because they earn more," says Michael Antecol, VP, Pollara. The statistics supported this statement. Only 30% of both middle-income and higher-income earners strongly agreed that they were saving more money now than they did five years ago. 55% of those earning less than $25,000 strongly disagreed with the statement.

On debt: Older respondents carried less debt. While 40% of eighteen-to-thirty-four-year-olds strongly agreed they had more debt than they did five years ago, this decreased to 30% for thirty-five-to forty-four year-olds, and to 18% for those aged fifty-five to sixty-four. Having children increased the debt carried. Again, income seems a minor factor in debt load. Very similar percentages of people from low-income and high-income earners carry debt. There was little gender difference in debt levels. Although females appeared to earn less, once they have money there is little difference in debt incurred.

On financial security: Interestingly younger respondents felt more financially secure than older respondents. Call it youthful naïveté or aged over-concern, but 50% of eighteen-to twenty-four-year-olds and 53% of twenty-five to thirty-four-year-olds very strongly agreed that they were more financially secure now than they were five years ago. Only 31% of those fifty-five to sixty-four and 24% of those sixty-five and older had the same confidence. The good news is that Vancouver, with the exclusion of the province of Alberta, had the highest financial security confidence of any area in the country. 39% of Vancouver respondents agreed very strongly that they were more financially secure than they were five years ago.

In response to an interest rate increase: We know that lines of credit have grown at a record pace in Canada, up 30% in 2004 alone. But a relatively low number of respondents admitted that a 2% interest rate increase would cause them concern. 15% of Vancouver respondents agreed strongly that they would be in trouble if interest rates increased 2%. Fully 50% disagreed with the statement. However, young women are a group to watch. 30% of women eighteen to thirty-four strongly agreed that an interest rate increase would put them in trouble. This difference may be the result of earning less than their male counterparts on average, but it is dramatically different than the male response of 15% admitting an interest rate increase would cause hardship.

So what does it all mean to marketers? Vancouverites are bullish. The economy appears strong and consumers perceive themselves to be managing debt and savings reasonably well. However, consumer perception doesn't always match consumer reality, and this may be the sleeper issue to watch. And there are many variations by age, income, and gender. It is there that the subtle, yet important, messages lie for those in the business of luring the consumer dollar.

In the Modern Marketplace, Time Is the New Currency

■ ■ ■

Business in Vancouver newspaper, December 20, 2005

"There never seems to be enough time to do the things you want to do once you find them." These words, taken from Jim Croce's 1973 hit "Time in a Bottle," resonate even stronger today than they did over thirty years ago. Year-end work stress, seasonal parties, shopping, and increased financial obligations all add up to less free time, less money in our pockets, and less sleep on the meter. But it's not just the holiday season with its increased stresses. The "time-starved" trend has been gaining momentum for some time now. The "value of time" is important to marketers, because time is the new currency.

Just how valuable is time? A recent Pollara study suggests - very valuable. In fact, well over half of BC respondents believed time was more valuable than money, with men and women ages thirty-five to fifty-four years agreeing most strongly with the statement. Considering this age group accounts for 31% of BC's population and holds considerable purchasing clout, marketers should take note. Think about that one the next time you consider reducing your prices for a sale. Perhaps you should be addressing the time efficiency of the customer interacting with your business. This second action might not be as easy to execute, but it is more likely to win you customer loyalty in the long run. This is the type of creative thinking required in an era where time has become more valuable to many than money.

Respondents were asked if they had less free time now than they did a year ago, as well as if they had less free time now than they did five years ago. Results indicate that there has been a dramatic loss of free time, and that the trend is building. But who do you think is the most time starved? The answer may surprise you. The study suggests males aged eighteen to thirty-four. 56% strongly agreed that they had less free time than they did five years ago. "People in this age group are huge multi-taskers, and multimedia has had a big impact on their lives. They do so much more than their age group did previously," suggests Michael Antecol, VP, Pollara. But "feeling overwhelmed by obligations to others" clearly belongs to women thirty-five to forty-four years, where one in three agreed strongly with the sentiment.

All of these results reinforce the increasing value being placed on time. Marketers must remember that the very act of browsing, comparing, and researching are time-intense activities. Even the process of filtering advertising messages involves time. Let's take a look at each of these steps in the marketing process with the view of being more time respectful.

1. Browsing: By its definition browsing is supposed to be relaxed and enjoyable. Yet with less disposable time available, you need to consider how to make browsing more efficient. Although some people may revel in the opportunity to rummage aimlessly for hours through products for a treasured find, most would prefer a "shopping sherpa" to help find the treasures. Sherpas guide, organize, and carry the load for mountaineers to make the journey easier. Apply this to your business. Think logical product organization, helpful displays, excellent signage, and knowledgeable, empowered staff. Offer the ability to do online research and pre-qualifying of products or services ahead of time. Think like a shopping sherpa. Browsing now is different than it used to be.

2. Research and comparison of product: The advent of the Internet and company websites has made this process much easier. From consumer reports and third-party research on products to actual comparison of competitor offerings, the web is utilized regularly for this purpose. Why not think like a customer and answer common questions? Do it in-store. Do it in your signage, in your brochures, and on your website. Arm your sales force with answers. Make your customers' research easier and more time efficient.

3. Filtering advertising messages: It is estimated that North Americans are exposed to more than 2,500 advertising messages daily. Take a moment and reflect. Of the messages you have seen or heard today, which are the ones you remember? They are likely the ones that you deemed timeworthy. Because in a time-starved world, what doesn't resonate gets discarded. Advertising only gains a recipient's time by providing desired information or by being entertaining. If it resonates, it's timeworthy. It will be remembered.

Time has become the new currency. We need to start considering the value of time in the marketing equation. And if you can figure out how to sell time in a bottle, that is where fortunes can be made.

A note to readers: Although time has become a valuable commodity, during an economic downturn traditionally consumers are willing to sacrifice time to save money. We are starting to see this trend now taking hold. Rather than paying a premium for time-saving pre-prepared meals or dining out, families are increasingly dining in to save money. Consumers are also now spending more time online researching the best deal prior to making a purchase. Expect this trend to continue with demographic groups most impacted by the economic downturn.

Playing the Value Game Is Vital in the New Shift-to-Thrift Era

■ ■ ■

Business in Vancouver newspaper, November 15, 2005

In my recent work with Pollara, the national public opinion and market research firm I've mentioned in other articles, we gathered information on consumer habits across Canada. We were particularly interested in purchase pattern changes over the last year and attitudes toward value, price, and quality. The findings revealed interesting implications for businesses and marketing professionals in particular.

In our survey of over 1,200 people across Canada, we asked if they were making fewer purchases now than a year ago, how likely they were to now delay purchases compared with a year ago, and the importance of price, quality, and value when making purchases. The patterns and attitudes conveyed reinforced the emergence of a "shift to thrift" trend.

A shift to thrift emerges when a population collectively looks for good value and becomes increasingly careful with their money.

There will always be price-sensitive shoppers, but as our study validated, they are likely to remain a minority. Overall, 38% of respondents agreed that price was the most important factor when purchasing consumer goods. Regionally, 33% in BC agreed with this statement, while 46% in Atlantic Canada did. Only 15% in BC "strongly agreed" with the statement. Of elevated importance was

CHAPTER 9 • TRENDS

the issue of quality. Overall, 66% of respondents agreed that quality was the most important factor when purchasing consumer goods. Regionally, 63% in BC agreed with this statement, and 29% "strongly agreed."

However, it was value that trumped the other two factors. Overall, 72% of respondents agreed that they always looked for the best value for the price paid when purchasing consumer goods. Regionally, 67% in BC agreed with this statement, while 76% in Atlantic Canada did. 37% in BC and 53% in Atlantic Canada "strongly agreed" with the statement. These are strong numbers.

When respondents were asked if they now make fewer purchases or are now delaying more purchases than they did a year ago, there were similar regional responses. Respondents in BC were among the nation's most bullish consumers. Overall, 29% of all respondents felt they were making fewer purchases of consumer goods now than a year ago. In BC this was 24%, and in Atlantic Canada 39% of respondents agreed with the statement. Overall, 34% of all respondents felt they were more likely to delay purchases now than one year ago. In BC this was 30%, and in Atlantic Canada 36% agreed with the statement. Age seemed a factor, with younger respondents feeling less likely to delay or make fewer purchases. The lower the education or income level, the greater the purchase apprehension. Urban respondents were decidedly more bullish in their purchase behaviours than rural respondents.

"Price is a factor, as is quality, but value is the most important factor. BC consumers appear to have a more bullish attitude about purchases, but even for them value is a key factor. You need to figure out what creates value for your target group to succeed in this market," says Michael Antecol, PhD and VP, Pollara.

The study confirmed that although there are regional and demographic differences in shopping behaviour, perceived value was of great importance to all respondents. What we are now seeing, and will likely see a lot more of in the future if this trend continues, is an increase in the "smart shopper," the one who seeks out the best value. This could mean increased consumer interest in getting the best deal on something desirable or wanting to get more for their money. It likely means an increase in consumers who want quality products that will last without paying a premium to get them. But a note of caution is in order. Value can mean different things to different people. Value can be determined by factors such as convenience, quality, selection, service, or price. In an era of shrinking disposable income, value for money has become very important.

Playing the value game will become critical in this era of "shift to thrift." For marketing it will be important to look at your target group and determine if there are specific offerings or services that would be of value to this group. Ideally, if you can isolate and offer something appealing and not currently available in your competitive marketplace, you will significantly boost your value equation and your overall business success.

Baby Boomers Are Leading the Shift-to-Thrift Trend

■ ■ ■

Business in Vancouver newspaper, September 20, 2005

Ghastly gas prices, an increase in the cost of goods across the board, and less disposable income at the end of day. This is likely to be our future. The pundits will no doubt shout that consumer spending is on the decline. They will say that the shift to thrift has arrived. But in reality, this trend has actually been entrenched for some time. Real incomes haven't grown much over the last decade, but consumer debt certainly has. 31% of BC's population are thirty-eight to fifty-seven-year-old baby boomers. This group is largely paying off mortgages, saving for or sending kids to post-secondary education, and saving for their own retirement. Collectively they are careful with their money and looking for good value. Although the boomers are only part of our population, as we all know, they have a significant impact on trends. The key to understanding the shift to thrift is to look at behaviours of this group and grasp that "good value" can mean many things other than the best price.

There will always be price-sensitive shoppers but they will likely remain a minority. What we are now seeing, and are likely to see a lot more in the future, is an increase in the "smart shopper," the one who seeks out the best value. And value means different things to different people. It may mean convenience, quality, selection, service, or price. In an era of shrinking disposable income, value for money will become very important.

This shift to thrift is not about buying the cheapest product. It's about getting the best deal on something desirable. It's about getting more for your money. And it's about buying quality products that will last without paying a premium to get them.

The shift to thrift has driven growth at big-box stores such as Home Depot, warehouse clubs such as Costco, high-end retail factory outlet stores, and quality discounters such as Winners. But what does this mean to marketers in general? Think *value, value, value.* And this goes well beyond just retail applications. This new value mantra applies to all commerce, both products and services.

The new-concept Canadian Tire stores are a great example. They are unlike any Canadian Tire you will remember from your youth, or suburbia for that matter. Oh sure, they still have automotive gear and tools, but you won't find them at the front of the store. And gone is the typical densely stacked merchandise displayed in narrow shopping aisles. These Canadian Tire stores feature mini boutique areas for sports clothing, paints, home décor, and gardening. Halogen lighting and hardwood floors in those sections create an urban, higher-end feel. The stores are vast, with over 60,000 square feet devoted to merchandising space. When was the last time you sat on a leather couch while waiting for your paint to be mixed? A sign noting "Too heavy? Too big? We deliver!" offers an unexpected service. They have effectively created a premium experience in a big-box format while preserving good prices and have effectively demonstrated a fundamental understanding of the shift to thrift.

The new-concept Home Depot stores are another good example. Although you can still find rows of tools and paint, you will also find the bath and kitchen boutiques, and a floor plan dramatically different from their traditional big-box format. The prices are still the same as the bargain large-format stores, but the feeling is of a premium experience. Again, they understand that the shift to thrift is all about creating value.

IGA Marketplace grocery stores are another example of a company that remade itself to capitalize on this trend. The stores feel high-end, with their warm lighting and market-style displays, when contrasted with traditional fluorescent-lit mega supermarkets. The message to the consumer is this: for about the same price as other grocery stores, you can have a premium experience. For many consumers this value makes them feel like they are getting more for their money. And that's right on target with the shift to thrift.

So in this new era you can play the price game with low margins, play the premium game and likely see business get increasingly tougher, or you can play the value game. This means creating a premium feel with superior service, convenience, selection, or quality. What offering can you make that is unique, desirable, or of premium quality, and do it at a fair price? What service or convenience can you offer that others are not? To win with the shift to thrift, these are the marketing questions you need to address.

Thank you for adding *Five-Minute Marketing* to your library. This book is the result of many years of professional experience as a marketing thought leader, speaker, writer, and strategist. I welcome your questions and insights. Email me at: mary@charleson.ca

Mary Charleson, May 2009

Presentations and keynotes

Have Mary deliver a marketing keynote, give a presentation, or conduct a workshop for your company. Mary is a member of the Canadian Association of Professional Speakers. Current topics:

> *The Female Factor: Gender Intelligent Marketing to Women*

> *Brands Giving Back: Social Strategy and Why It's Good Business to Do Good*

> *Tips, Trends and Takeaways: Savvy Marketing Advice for Women in Business*

> *Effective Advertising: Use Your Precious Budget Wisely*

> *Sins, Staples and Small Pleasures: How to Survive and Thrive in a Down Economy.*

Keynotes can be specialized for your industry. Contact Mary to discuss your needs.

Get marketing insights delivered to your inbox
Visit www.charleson.ca and sign up for *Marketing Rapport*, an e-newsletter about marketing trends and research.

Join the conversation:
Visit Mary's blog www.fiveminutemarketing.com and share your thoughts on a variety of marketing topics.

Consulting services

If you are interested in consulting services, contact us. Let's talk!
Charleson Communications
Vancouver (604) 990-1516
Email: mary@charleson.ca
or visit: www.charleson.ca

Satisfied clients get the last word!

"One of the best presentations we've ever had. There was a lot
of interest from our members on this topic, *Effective Advertising:
How to Use Your Budget Wisely*. Mary certainly delivered."
- Dianna Hambrook, Events Manager, Burnaby Board of Trade.

"Mary's presentation was the highest rated at our Branding
Conference in Toronto! It addressed branding, the brand promise,
and social strategy. Attendees found the session to be extremely
well presented and filled with exciting as well as tangible examples."
- Kevin Strychalski, Conference Planner, Federated Press

"Mary's Special Interest Group Session *Marketing to Women* was
sold out. BCAMA member feedback was fantastic. A compelling
topic very well presented. She was one of our best speakers this year."
- Evangeline Englezos, 2005/06 BCAMA President

"Mary's presentation *Delivering on Your Brand Promise* offered great
insights into social strategy. We were pleased to have Mary back to
speak to our chapter again this year."
- Laura McBride, 2006/07 BCAMA President

"If your business relies on decisions made by women, and it
appears most do, then you can't afford to miss the *Marketing to
Women* presentation. Mary breaks down the top ten things you need
to know to successfully market to women in a simple but profound

manner using an interesting mix of statistics, interviews, and other multimedia demonstrations. One of our most successful and well attended events this season!"
- Heather Knittel, Chair, BC Chapter Canadian Women in Communication

"Mary's presentation to the Canadian Women in Communication on marketing to women was excellent. She was able to convey an important message and honour both men and women, which is sometimes hard to do."
- Maureen Fitzgerald, PhD, LLM, LLB, BComm, Lawyer and President, CenterPoint Conflict & Collaboration

"Mary's presentation *Marketing to Baby Boomer Women* was extremely enlightening."
- Avis Sokol, Director, Relationship Marketing, Vancity

"A simple but inspirational message on connecting with women. Engaging, humorous, and very informative."
- Lynne Zlotnik Wealth Management

"Fabulous! Everyone thoroughly enjoyed the morning presentation."
- Gabrielle Loren, President, SWAN, Successful Women Always Network

"Lots of relevant examples that could be applied to my business."
- Attendee, 4th Annual Marketing to Moms Conference, Toronto

"Inspiring and fact-based presentation."
- Kim Alke, Brand Analyst, Rogers Communications

"Great statistics, very engaging presenter - knowledgeable yet still approachable. Loved the Vancity example."
- Tracy Fay-Powers, Manager, Creative Development, Farm Credit Canada

"Entertaining and informative. Mary certainly delivered."
- Camille Rosen, Health Care Leaders of BC Conference 2007, Vancouver

"Thank you for moderating our panel *Women in Advertising*. The feedback was excellent."

- *Cindy Goldrick, Events Director, Women's Executive Network*

"Your presentation *Branding and Positioning* was fabulous. Very valuable, complete and informative."

- *Shauna Gnutel, Director, YMCA New Ventures Network*

"Your presentations *Effective Advertising* and *E-marketing* were a great addition to our annual conference."

- *Susan Stevenson, Executive Director, Greater Vancouver Professional Theatre Alliance*